THE ONLY
PIRATE
AT THE
PARTY

THE ONLY PIRATE AT THE PARTY

LINDSEY STIRLING

AND

BROOKE S. PASSEY

GALLERY BOOKS

NEW YORK   LONDON   TORONTO   SYDNEY   NEW DELHI

G

Gallery Books
An Imprint of Simon & Schuster, Inc.
1230 Avenue of the Americas
New York, NY 10020

First Gallery Books hardcover edition January 2016

GALLERY BOOKS and colophon are registered trademarks of Simon & Schuster, Inc.

For information about special discounts for bulk purchases, please contact Simon & Schuster Special Sales at 1-866-506-1949 or business@simonandschuster.com.

The Simon & Schuster Speakers Bureau can bring authors to your live event. For more information or to book an event, contact the Simon & Schuster Speakers Bureau at 1-866-248-3049 or visit our website at www.simonspeakers.com.

Manufactured in the United States of America

10   9   8   7   6   5   4   3   2   1

Library of Congress Cataloging-in-Publication Data

Stirling, Lindsey, 1986-
  The only pirate at the party / Lindsey Stirling and Brooke S. Passey.—First Gallery Books hardcover edition.
    pages cm
  1. Stirling, Lindsey, 1986- 2. Violinists—United States—Biography. 3. Composers—United States—Biography. I. Passey, Brooke S. II. Title.
  ML418.S77A3 2016
787.2092—dc23   [B]   2015030510

ISBN 978-1-5011-1910-1
ISBN 978-1-5011-1918-7 (ebook)

NOTE TO READERS: Names of certain people portrayed have been changed, whether or not noted as such.

For the dreamers who gave me life,
I love you Mammy and Pappy.

And for the dreamers who gave my music life,
my beautiful fans.

CONTENTS

ONE
THE CHILDHOOD/DEVELOPING TEENAGER PART

Be yourself; everyone else is already taken.

—OSCAR WILDE

CROSS YOUR EYES AND DOT YOUR TEES: A PIRATE'S INTRO

I didn't learn to read until I was halfway through the first grade. Reading was work—hard work, and not the rewarding kind. For years, I struggled through reading at school, doing so slower and with longer vowels than anyone else. This befuddled my mother. I was a pretty sharp kid in all other aspects of life. I was a math whiz, a science pro, relatively talented with my violin, and I could repeat the facts I learned on *Sesame Street* from memory. Why couldn't I read? At the end of second grade, I was still phonetically sounding out *basketball*, so she took me in for some testing. When the results came back, the doctor pulled my mom aside and told her I had a learning disability referred to as cross dominance. Cross what? I know, you've never heard of it before, either. But it's a real thing. In case you don't want to google it, I'll give you the skinny.

Most people have a dominant half. Meaning, information goes in primarily through the dominant eye or ear, processes in the brain, and comes out instructing the dominant side of the body to perform a correlating motor function. For example, when someone sees a soccer ball information processes mostly through the dominant eye, and the brain tells the dominant leg to kick the ball. Oftentimes, people with cross dominance mix up these signals, and use alternating sides of the body instead of a consistently dominant one. Cross dominance also affects the way the brain processes cognitive functions. A normal person reads as follows: the dominant eye sees the word *matriculation*, information processes mostly on the dominant side of the brain, and the mouth says *matriculation*. In my case, the left eye sees the word *matriculation*, it goes into my brain where the signals get passed around and switched up, and it comes out my mouth *bran muffin*. I don't know, ask my doctor. Basically, it's a lot like dyslexia, only completely different. Anyway, with this new knowledge, it was recommended that I undergo eye therapy a few times a week to help my nondominant eye catch up, and maybe teach my brain how to process information in a more organized manner. I was also given a series of exercises to do at home during the week. This included the task of wearing an eye patch over my dominant eye for an hour every day. Oh, the agony!

Wearing the eye patch was awful. Until one day I came across a disposable pirate hat in my closet, and it clicked. I wasn't a weird girl stuck in an eye patch, I was a pirate stuck in a weird suburban backyard. From that time forward I spent at least an hour every day turning the swing set into a giant pirate ship, where I played Cap'n Davy and made my sister and our friend Mary walk the plank.

Arrr! Even after the mandatory eye patch time came to an end, my fascination with the swashbuckling riffraff remained. Pirates rarely shower, have a random and effortlessly cool sense of style, and if you turn a blind eye to all the plundering, they are really just in search of "treasure." I can relate to all these things. More than anything, though, I have always admired the pirate attitude. Pirates don't take orders or ask permission. They do what they want. Allow me to clarify. If your mom asks you to do the dishes, DO NOT pull out your pirate attitude. But if someone tells you you're not good enough, says your dreams are too lofty, or claims there is no room in showbiz for a dancing violinist—well then, by all means, pull out your eye patch, my friend, and take to the high seas. (That's my way of saying do it anyway.) The reason people said I would never succeed is the very reason I did succeed: because I am different. That's not to say I've tried to stand out, but when given the choice between being a weird kid in an eye patch or a pirate, the answer was easy. I want to say it is still easy, but I can't lie to you like that. Sometimes being the only pirate is hard. And that's okay, too.

With the help of Cap'n Davy's accessory, my reading improved over the years, but I still spell worse than the average bear. Anyone who follows me on social media knows this to be true. My fans are constantly screen-grabbing my spelling errors—it's a little game they play. Luckily, my trusty spellcheck and an even trustier editor assure me I won't embarrass myself in the pages you hold now. (My editor asked me to clarify that this refers only to spelling mistakes, and he cannot protect me from any other form of embarrassment in this book.) Po-tay-to, po-tah-to! Shall we get this party started?

A GIRL
IN CURLS

As a child, I had a big head, a tiny voice, and a total disregard for social cues. All young kids are oblivious at first—public tantrums and soiling one's pants are somehow okay in infancy—but eventually most children start noticing and mimicking cultural norms. I, on the other hand, managed to glide through childhood without perceiving (or perhaps caring about) these "accepted behaviors." To be clear, my mother tells me I stopped pooping my pants at a very early age, but she also told me not to use any form of the word *poop* in my book. Anyway, I just never seemed to care much about what other people were doing.

I was a natural-born drama queen, and my kindergarten classroom set the stage for one of my earliest impromptu performances. One morning as I was getting dressed for school I found myself digging through boxes of dress-up clothes instead of my dresser. And to think, all this time I'd been limiting the use of costumes to playdates and Halloween—what a waste!

Minutes later, I emerged from my room wearing a kimono, red sequined shoes, a single glove, and a curly brown wig. Had the wig been red I would have been overjoyed—Little Orphan Annie was one of my first idols—but this wig would do. It had short, uneven ringlets, and if I shifted my weight just so, I could make the frizzy curls dance around my face. The cute outfit my mother had purchased for the first day of school lay in a heap on my bedroom floor. When I announced to her that I was ready for school, she took one bemused look at me and did what any good mother would do—she handed me my lunch and drove me to Jefferson Elementary.

When I arrived, my class was already gathered for Circle Time, reading quietly on the opposite side of the room. To draw their attention I walked through the door, spread my arms wide, and struck the most dramatic pose I could think of. "Tada!" I said in a mouse-like voice as I hopped from one spindly leg to the other. The class erupted into giggles, and I felt like a champion. Mrs. Fowler wasted no time in sending for the principal—but only so she could showcase her slightly odd student.

Despite my larger-than-life theatrics, I was always quite small for my age. In the first grade, I compensated by becoming best friends with two giants named Krista and Naomi. Maybe their tall-girl instincts told them I needed looking after, or maybe I subconsciously gravitated to their protective body types; either way, we made a wicked team.

Here we are on a field trip to the petting zoo, Krista and Naomi mean muggin' the camera in my defense.

On second thought, maybe it was our mutual love for saggy denim that brought us together.

Krista and Naomi's parents were also best friends, so they were constantly doing things together outside of school. After a few months of playing with them at recess, the girls brought me into their inner circle of friendship by inviting me to Knott's Berry Farm. When Naomi asked me if I wanted to go with her I was speechless. Going to Knott's Berry Farm was considered a full-fledged vacation for my family. Apparently, to hers it was an average weekend activity, one to which she could invite friends no less!

When Naomi's mom called that night I could hear my mom in the next room.

"Hi Clair, I was just thinking we needed to invite Naomi over again soon."

There was a pause.

"Oh, are you sure? Okay." My mom continued, "Thank you, she is going to be so excited."

And just like that it was settled.

On the morning of our outing I slipped into my best saggy jeans and waited anxiously for my ride by the front door. As I sat looking out the window my mom watched from the kitchen.

"Lindsey, are you excited to go to Knott's Berry Farm?" she asked.

"Yes," I said smiling, eagerly looking for Naomi's red SUV.

"I want you to tell me about all the rides when you get back. Maybe another time we'll go together."

"Okay," I replied, my focus unwavering.

My mom, like most, wanted to give her kids everything and more. But she was also the kind of mom who never spent money she didn't have. If we ran out of milk before the end of the month, we ate Cream of Wheat instead of cereal; and when we ate a lot of Cream of Wheat, we didn't go places like the local Blockbuster, let alone Knott's Berry Farm.

"Hey Lindsey, look at me for a second."

Reluctantly, I turned toward my mom. She was smiling gently.

"You know I love you, right?"

"Yep," I said quickly, but I was immediately distracted by the slow crunch of tires pulling into the driveway.

"She's here!" I screamed, jumping up and running for the door.

"All right, have fun!" she yelled back, scrubbing a pan in the sink.

Soon after arriving at the amusement park, we realized I wasn't tall enough for the most exciting rides. I frequently got left behind with Naomi's younger brother, Troy. At first I was disappointed—how was I going to tell my mom about the rides if I couldn't even get on them? But eventually Naomi's mom started buying Troy and me special treats to keep us occupied. All I had to do was look at something for longer than six seconds and she would offer to buy it: cotton candy, churros, frozen lemonade, fry bread, and endless turns at the ring toss booth. The wonders of concession stand food were new to me. Usually, when we went out, my mom packed sandwiches that became soggy in her purse by lunchtime. Naomi's mom had obviously forgotten to make lunches, which was okay, since she seemed to have an endless supply of five-dollar bills to fill their place.

At one point, Naomi's mom suggested that the girls go on a smaller ride with Troy and me. Naomi looked back and forth between her mother and Krista before she replied, "But those rides are boring." I waited for Naomi's mom to pull her daughter aside to have a chat about being polite and, I don't know, *a good friend*. Instead, she handed me another five-dollar bill and let the girls go on their way.

Before long I was stuffed, but the more I ate, the more I wanted. There was no telling when I would get another opportunity to have so much processed food and sugar, or win such ugly (but giant!) stuffed animals again. So I kept looking, and eating, and playing the ring toss. When I returned home at the end of the day I felt sick. But I was delighted by the hideous stuffed lizard under my arm. So what if I'd spent the entire day with a four-year-old boy?

Over time Krista and Naomi introduced me to other things: the Miss America Pageant, eating at restaurants for no particular reason, and the idea of getting paid for doing chores. They called that one "allowance," and they were both shocked to hear I had never received one.

"What do you mean you don't get paid to clean your room?"

I was also surprised to find out that a different tooth fairy visits rich people. One time Naomi received five dollars for a front tooth. One tooth! It wasn't even that big. In fact, Naomi had tiny teeth—the kind of teeth that barely reached the cob when she ate corn. I, on the other hand, had beaver cleavers, and I was certain they were going to work in my favor. The next time I lost a tooth I asked Naomi if she would put it under *her* pillow, which she did, and I eagerly awaited my grand prize. Her fairy was going to be so impressed. The next day she returned with the tooth but no cash. Her fairy didn't buy it. Disappointed, I put it under my pillow and awoke the next morning to find two shiny quarters in its place. I imagined my little fairy carrying those quarters through the night, one under each arm (which would have been much harder to fly with than a five-dollar bill), and I was grateful for her extra effort—even if the amount of money was a letdown. At breakfast that morning my mom handed me a bowl of Cream of Wheat and sat down at the table.

"So, did the tooth fairy come last night?" she asked.

I considered telling her about Naomi's five dollars, but I was worried she might call the Tooth Fairy Office to complain, and what if my fairy got fired? I kept it to myself and answered, "Yes, I got two quarters."

"Two whole quarters? That must have been one big tooth!"

Tell that to Naomi's fairy, I thought. But the more I thought about it, the more I appreciated my fairy's quarters. She wasn't the richest, obviously, but she was definitely one of the strongest. I liked my little fairy, she did good.

MIND YOUR
OWN BUSINESS

Shortly after my eighth birthday, my dad was hired as a high school religion teacher in Mesa, Arizona. When the topic of our impending move was brought up, I think it worried my mom that I didn't shed a single tear over the idea of saying good-bye to Krista and Naomi. I guess deep down I couldn't relate that well to anyone who kept their toys in glass cases.

The day after we moved into our new home Dawnee Ray came to our door at 7:00 A.M., with bare feet and a wagon full of lemons. She was my height with tangled hair only a few shades darker than her olive skin.

"Hi, I'm Dawnee. My mom told me to give these to you."

She pointed at the wagon of fruit behind her.

"Thanks, I'm Lindsey."

She held out a thin, tan hand, "Nice to meet you, Linseed."

Dawnee never called anything by its rightful name. A wheelbarrow was a "wobbler," cookies were "cooklets," and I was any number of names that started with the letter L. Over the course of our friendship, I was "Lizard," "Lindy Hop," "Lindizzle," and "Limesey Styling," to name a few. Her refusal to use correct terminology annoyed many of her siblings, but being friends with Dawnee was the best thing that ever happened to my imagination.

As it turned out, she was equally deprived in the allowance department. Instead of complaining, she convinced me that we should take moneymaking matters into our own hands. Our first attempt: the lemonade stand.

I never understood advertisements that drew attention to the lack of key ingredients: *now with 30 percent less sugar*. Why would anyone admit that? Whenever I tried to sneak food into my mom's grocery cart I was careful to avoid those kinds of treats—I was no fool. So when Dawnee and I decided to go into the lemonade stand business, we took a different approach. We squeezed forty-six lemons, added the magic ingredient with a generous hand, and made a poster that read: LEMONADE, NOW WITH 30% MORE SUGAR! Then we took a walk down to the end of our street and set up shop across from the cornfields, where approximately three cars passed every hour. Yes, I said *passed*. We sat there, sipping on lemon syrup and talking about how delicious it was until we were too sick to sit up straight.

As we were packing up, Dawnee's mom drove down the street and cheerfully asked if we were still in business. She handed us a dime, and I handed her a tall glass of warm lemonade. We waited, proudly watching our only customer of the day take a big sip. She gently lowered her cup and asked us how much sugar we used. From the moment we answered onward, Dawnee and I were only allowed to make lemonade under supervision.

Another one of our failed moneymakers was Movie Night. We

made cookies and popcorn, and created personalized placemats. For only two dollars, all three could be yours! Our older sisters always had babysitting money, but they were never going to give it to us. One Saturday before a viewing of *The Shaggy D.A.*, Dawnee's older sister Sherri walked up to our concession stand at the kitchen counter. She placed her hands on the granite, cocked her hip to the side, and examined our goods.

"How much for one of those burnt cookies?"

Dawnee looked hurt. "They're not burnt—"

"Fifty cents," I cut in before the argument escalated. I was willing to take anything.

"Too much," Sherri said.

And with that she walked to the cupboard, grabbed a bag of popcorn, and put it in the microwave herself. I wanted to call attention to the injustice, but Dawnee turned the other cheek. "It won't taste as good as ours. We added a secret ingredient," she said proudly.

Sherri grinned. "I'm not sure if extra butter counts as a secret, but it could certainly pass for disgusting."

Our only interested buyers ended up being my younger sister Brooke and Dawnee's younger sister Heidi, and of course they didn't have any money. Eventually, we ended up paying them a quarter each to clean up the kitchen, which they gave back a few minutes later in exchange for a small bag of popcorn and half a cookie. We threw in their placemats for free since we had already decorated them.

A few months later, my school started their annual candy bar fund-raiser. After the motivational speech, involving a slideshow of outrageous prizes, I was determined to win the mini-fridge *and* a bike. According to the motivational sales guy, "It would only take twenty thousand orders," or something like that. Notwithstanding my zealous attitude, I returned my catalogue the next week with two orders—one from Mrs. Boyle down the street, and the other from Sherri Ray. It turns out she did have a soft heart; it was simply hidden beneath a mound of overpriced holiday chocolate.

The Ready-To-Work Girls was a third Lindsey-Dawnee enterprise that was eventually quite a success. We made business cards and distributed them throughout the neighborhood, advertising our services for basically anything. WE'LL DO YOUR JOB FOR YOUR PRICE. Sometimes we got lucky and a generous benefactor would overpay us, but more often than not, we got royally ripped off.

One of our most reliable customers was Mr. Hult. He was a portly man, to put it kindly, and every day he wore a starched button-up. When we first advertised our services at his door, he handed us five shirts, a can of starch, and offered us a dollar for every one we ironed. At first this seemed like a great deal—until we tried ironing one of his shirts and realized it was a time-consuming and sweat-producing chore. Did I mention Mr. Hult was a size infinity? I mean, the guy was short, but the more I ironed his shirts the more I was convinced I could use them as bedsheets. Every time we returned his shirts he handed us five more, and my heart sank. Sometimes I thought about leaving the wrinkled shirts on the doorstep and making a run for it. Instead, Dawnee and I took turns starching and ironing, starching and ironing . . .

Then there were people like Patty Miller down the street who called for our services and paid us in half-consumed boxes of food. Even with the warm, fuzzy feeling that comes from helping an elderly woman, I wasn't quite satisfied with a few bags of fruit snacks and a box of Cheerios in return for three hours of yard work. After doing this a few times, I tried to convince Dawnee that we didn't have to answer every time Patty called.

"I mean, if she doesn't pay well enough we don't have to keep going back. We could just say we're busy . . ."

Dawnee listened, neither agreeing nor disagreeing.

A few days later, Dawnee called and I got to the phone as she was leaving a message.

"Hi Limesey, it's Dawnee. Patty called. There are some weeds in her flower garden that she can't reach. It's okay if you can't make it today, but I'm going over there now."

There was no good reason I wouldn't be able to make it, and Dawnee knew that. Her refusal to acknowledge my selfish attitude left me feeling more ashamed than any formal reprimand could have. Dawnee would never openly tell me I was wrong, but her message was a quiet invitation to change my mind. She was going to help Patty with or without me, so I grabbed my gloves and ran outside. She was already halfway up the street, carrying a small shovel and dragging a rake behind her, its teeth collecting stray rocks and sticks from the pavement as she walked.

"Hey Dawnsey!" I called as I jogged toward her. "Wait up!"

She turned and smiled.

"Here, take this rattle bagger," she said, handing me the rake.

Since I know you're all wondering, we got paid that day with polar punch popsicles. They made our mouths turn blue, so Dawnee called me "Sal" and accused me of stealing all her berries. I thought it was hilarious, and we giggled the entire walk home.

*Thanks, Dawnee, for teaching me how to work hard
and be kind; and for showing me how to properly pose
for the camera—belly out, hand limp.*

SAVE THE
WHALES!

The summer of ninety-six was one of the best my neighborhood had ever seen. For starters, Hunter Spalding got in trouble for accidentally setting fire to his kitchen and had to spend the entirety of May, June, and July digging up rusty fence posts in his front yard. He was a bad boy with good hair and the face of a baby angel. Dawnee and I were nine and he was three years our senior, but that didn't stop us from "casually" riding our bikes past his house every five minutes. Lucky for us, it was also the year that Brooke and Heidi took a liking to horses. We convinced them to be our majestic steeds by pulling us around the neighborhood in a garden cart for hours at a time. We gave them lavish names like Black Ebony and Star Dancer, and fed them carrots until they thought *we* were doing *them* a favor.

Once we had them trained, we commanded them to pull us past

Hunter's yard. We stood in the back of the cart like Roman chariot-eers as Brooke and Heidi struggled to pull us slowly along, Dawnee and I nodding nonchalantly as we passed. If the way we'd enslaved our sisters didn't impress him, the boys' department cargo shorts we were wearing certainly would. That summer was also the year I became secretary for the NAAEC—the Nature, Animal, and Environment Club.

The neighborhood obsession with animals all started with my sister Jennifer. One of the things I loved most about her back then was her Ranger Rick animal-page collection. Each month, a new page arrived in the mail and she would place it gently into an alphabetized binder. Sometimes, she let Brooke and me sit next to her while she read through all the facts within the shiny bifold, so long as we didn't touch the pages. The pictures were so vibrant, I wanted to rub my hands all over them. When Jennifer wasn't home, I occasionally took the binder out from under her bed and flipped through the pictures. The blue-footed booby was my favorite. It really is a beautiful bird, but mostly I liked any excuse to say the word *booby*.

One day a humpback whale page came in the mail, and Jennifer read aloud the tragic statistics on survival rates. The room fell silent, Brooke got teary, and Jennifer said solemnly, "We have to do something."

This was before the days of Google, so Jennifer called the customer service number on the back of the page. She waited on hold for two hours and twenty-three minutes, got transferred around for another hour, and finally got the name of an organization that protects whales. When she emerged from her room three and a half hours later, Brooke and I had long forgotten about the cause. In fact, whales annoyed me a little. *If you need air to survive then what are you doing living under water, anyway?!* But Jennifer was determined, and trying to change her mind once she was set on something was like trying to discuss sandwich boundaries with a ravenous goose.

"We're going to adopt a humpback whale," she said matter-of-factly.

It sounded great in theory, but where were we going to keep a pet whale? I decided to let her figure out the details and agreed to help. Jennifer explained her plan.

"The lady on the phone said it's thirty dollars a year to adopt a whale. If we each put in twenty-five cents a week, we can save a whale in ten months . . . but if we can get ten people to donate twenty-five cents a week, we will have enough money in three months."

It sounded simple enough, but I still wasn't sure how we were going to persuade ten people to donate a quarter for the upkeep of an air-breathing water dweller every week. Naturally, Jennifer had a solution for that too.

"We need to start a club," she said.

And that was the start of the Nature, Animal, and Environment Club. Once we had a name, the recruitment process began. First stop: the Rays' house.

Dawnee's family lived across the street with a houseful of kids and a yard full of cows, chickens, bunnies, pigeons, and cats—it was a no-brainer. Also, the fact that Dawnee and her two sisters were our best friends and accomplices in all things irrational guaranteed us a weekly seventy-five-cent contribution. We also convinced the Heydt kids, Rebecca Crum, and Megan Boyle to join. Hunter Spalding even came to one of our meetings, but after my fascinating presentation on the water beetle, he never returned. One of life's great mysteries.

The NAAEC went on for some time. Jennifer was president, the brains, and the researcher behind all our projects; Sherri was vice president, only because she was the next oldest and Jennifer's best friend; Dawnee was the treasurer, due to her impeccable organizational skills; and I was the secretary—because that was the only position left. Brooke and Heidi begged for titles, so we labeled them townspeople. They took it much better than we expected.

After a few months we decided our weekly meetings weren't bringing in enough quarters, so Jennifer came up with the brilliant idea of putting on a play and charging the audience (our parents) admission. The production was called "Animals Fight For Freedom," and it was written, directed, and starred in by—you guessed it—me. My favorite scene was the one where I turned the couch into a boat, stood on the bow, and gave a moving speech about "helping the underdogs." Another personal highlight was when I waved our club flag back and forth yelling, "Save the blue-footed boobies!" It never got old. I think we made close to ten dollars, and we were ecstatic. Eventually, we not only adopted a whale but had also saved enough money to protect two and a half feet of rain forest. I know it has made some centipede very happy.

Me, Dawnee, Brooke, and Heidi in matching club shirts, acid-washed jeans, and bowler hats . . . it made sense at the time.

you're Invited

The Animal Club's Talent Show

Come see Sherri Ray and Jennifer Stirling do a crazy leg dance, Heidi Ray and Brooke Stirling tell their favorite jokes, Lindsey Stirling and Dawnee Ray square dance, and perform with Megan Boyle, Rebecca Crum do all of the announcing and the whole club sing two spectacular songs written by Lindsey Stirling.

Date: June 28th
Time: 7:00 - 7:45 PM
Place: The Stirlings Home
Bring: JUST YOURSELVES!

There will be refreshments!

PUT THE CANDY
IN THE POUCH

Third grade was a big year for me. I placed first in the science fair with an experiment involving potatoes and electricity, and I designed my first homemade Halloween costume. Given the endless amount of dress-up clothes in the basement, picking a costume should have been a breeze. Being a bit of a forward thinker, though, I was never satisfied with a costume in which I'd already played house. My mom is an excellent seamstress, and the weeks leading up to Halloween found her glued to a chair in front of her sewing machine—either altering existing costumes or making new ones. That year as the holiday grew closer, I decided I would take a turn in the hot seat. I thought of the perfect costume, sketched a pattern, and proudly declared I was going to make a kangaroo suit—if not for the sheer challenge, then definitely for the secret candy pouch. No amount of gentle suggestions that I "start with something simpler" could convince me otherwise, so my mom took me down to Sally's Fabrics and helped me find four yards of brown furry fabric.

"Just as long as you know this is going to be difficult and will take a lot of work," she said on the drive over.

My mom could have saved a lot of time and money by just saying no to my request. But because she never told me I wouldn't be able to do it, I did it. That's the best part about being a kid. Nothing seems impossible until someone bigger and older tells you it is. I grew up in a lovely little world where nothing was too far out of reach if I wanted to work for it. I think I still live in that world.

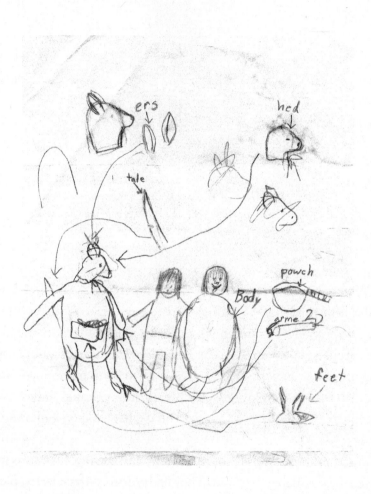

The finished product had a few minor flaws—mainly that I couldn't breathe, and I spent the entire night tripping over my very realistic kangaroo feet—but the good news is I was the only kangaroo on the block that year (or any year, as far as I know).

Note to future costume designers: Make sure you don't sew the se-
cret candy pouch too low, because then it looks like you're pulling
candy from your saggy Kanga-crotch . . . and people don't find that
cute, no matter how long it took to sew the dang thing on.

When the Ty Beanie Baby craze hit Gilbert, Arizona, I was in the fifth grade, and looking hard for my next creative outlet. I bought Pinky the Flamingo off a grocery store endcap. A few days later Brooke picked up Chocolate the Moose because I wouldn't stop bragging about how cool Pinky was. It started out innocent enough, just the two of us and the two of them. But as Beanie Babies grew in popularity, Brooke and I jumped on the bandwagon and hung on for dear life.

For hours at a time, we sat in the basement sewing intricate outfits for our Beanie Babies by hand. They had ruffled skirts, pleated pants, collared shirts, and veiled hats. They came with names but once they were in our possession we paired them up and married them off, based on appearance, lifestyle, and our own matchmaker intuition. Not only did they have nice clothes and families, they also held jobs and participated in regular town meetings, in which new Beanies were introduced and other important Beanie business was attended to. McDonald's Happy Meal Teenie Beanies afforded our Beanie couples the joys of having children. They were more functional than the average American family. This went on till the end of my sixth grade year.

Nowadays, most sixth graders wear makeup and conduct important social business on smartphones. When I was in sixth grade I was wearing some hand-me-down overalls and conducting important social business among my Beanie Babies. Same thing, right?

I wanted to include a picture of one of my Beanie outfits, but I couldn't find any. I did, however, find this Mother's Day marionette I made when I was nine. What mother doesn't want a saggy-bottomed ostrich puppet in honor of the biggest sacrifice of her life? I know my mom did, or at least that's what she told me when I presented it to her.

ON OLDER
SISTERS

Before we moved to Arizona, Jennifer and I spent most of our free time at Bianca and Leanne's house. Or should I say Biancaandleanne's house. They were twins, the kind you'd imagine on the Disney Channel, and I don't remember ever addressing one without the other. I was about seven at the time, Jennifer was ten, and Biancaandleanne were nine. It would have been a perfect recipe for friendship had Jennifer and I gotten along. Because we were about as compatible as a Q-tip and a bowling ball, Jennifer spent most of her time trying to convince the twins to lose me.

I prided myself on my ability to keep up with Jennifer when she didn't want me around—partly because I liked being included and partly because I liked annoying her. In fact, I think bothering Jennifer was the first thing in life I excelled at. She had a fiery temper, and setting her off was almost too easy. Once, after watching an episode of *Sesame Street* about sharing, Jennifer took it upon herself to teach me the importance of taking turns. She handed me the most coveted toy in the house, a purple-tailed My Little Pony. Then she sweetly asked if I would like to trade her for Gus, the Breyer horse who was missing three of his four legs. Of course I took one look at the crippled Gus and flatly replied, "No."

Jennifer tried again. "Lindsey, will you *please* share your pony?"

"No."

At this point her gentle request turned into a forceful grab that ended in a customary episode of tug-of-war and screaming.

"YOU NEED TO SHARE!"

We pulled and screamed until the poor little pony's head popped right off. Although I was partially to blame for this one, Jennifer was always breaking things—toys, plates, her wrists (that's another story)—but my point? The girl could pack a punch.

Several of Jennifer's friends also had younger siblings—most frequently brothers—who were forced upon me for playdates. One day, after playing Teenage Mutant Ninja Princess, Michael and I went looking for our older sisters. They were hiding from us as usual, and during our search we overheard them talking behind some boxes in the garage.

"Lindsey is so annoying. I would trade her for Michael any day," Jennifer said.

"You can have Michael. I'd rather have a younger sister than a brother," her friend replied.

"No, you don't want Lindsey."

We stood in front of the garage, listening to our sisters talk us down. Michael looked like he might cry, but I remember thinking, *Oh yeah? You think I'm annoying now?* I always loved a challenge.

In the beginning, Jennifer had wanted to be my big sister. The Halloween after I was born, my mom dressed us up as Tom and Jerry—two boys who hate each other—but regardless of the deeper implications of our costumes, Jennifer was very proud of me that year. According to my parents, anytime someone complimented Jennifer's costume she pointed at me in my mom's arms and said, "Yes, but look at the mouse!" I too fell easily into my role as the younger sister at first, following Jennifer around and trying to do everything she did. Once, she snuck some holiday chocolate from my parents' room, and to prove my allegiance I willingly took the blame. When my mom found the wrapper on the floor, she gathered the two of us in the kitchen.

"Who took this candy bar from my room and ate it?"

Surely my mom knew who it was based on the chocolate smeared around Jennifer's mouth, but she wanted to offer the chance to come clean. To her surprise it was I who confessed.

"I did it," I said in a small voice.

My mom looked me in the eye. "Lindsey, are you sure *you* ate the candy bar?"

"Yes."

I was stone-cold serious. Jennifer smiled innocently, and a crumb of chocolate flaked off the corner of her mouth. My mom sighed, *So this is how it's going to be.*

And that's how it was . . . for a while. I hated pizza because Jennifer wouldn't eat it, and I loved orange sorbet because it was her favorite. But Jennifer was very controlling by nature, so we only got along if I agreed with everything she said. Eventually, I realized I had a few opinions of my own—mostly that I didn't want to play with Gus anymore. Once Brooke was old enough to play with me,

Twenty bucks says you didn't notice Jennifer was in this picture.
Don't blame me; the tree costume was her idea! But this
picture pretty adequately sums up our childhood.

it was game over. I wasn't just the younger sister anymore; I was an older sister now, too. Eventually, I started refusing to play Jennifer's games her way, which frustrated her to no end. So began the clash of our personalities that lasted through high school.

When my mom first tried to explain the term *depression* to me, I was seven. I already knew Jennifer liked to be alone, that she was irritable and short-tempered, and that she didn't think I was funny. But the thought that someone could be sad for no reason didn't make sense to me. As I got older I learned to accept her depression as a reality, but she was difficult to be around, and I never tried to make it any easier on her. We grew up, and we grew apart.

Although we weren't the best of friends growing up, we did come together out of necessity on occasion. Once, during an argument, I threw a broom at her. I missed (on purpose!) and it punctured a hole in her bedroom door instead. We gasped in unison, and the argument was over as quickly as it had started. She pulled the broom from the door and I cut an appropriately sized circle out of a shoebox. Together, we painted it to match the existing wood grain and taped it over the hole. Then we stood back and looked over our handiwork.

"She won't notice, will she?" I asked.

"Not a chance."

My mom didn't notice the hole until we pointed it out to her years later—teamwork at its finest. But, more often than not, we were at odds.

When she was a teenager, nothing was more important to Jennifer than running, and for good reason. In junior high she broke the school record for the mile, and by the time she was a high school sophomore her face was showing up in every local newspaper: STIRLING TAKES FIRST or SOPHOMORE FOR STATE. As the season progressed, neighbors kept bringing their clippings to our house. This was partially because they knew we didn't get the paper, and also because my mom sent out a mass e-mail asking for them. After we had a sizable pile by the door, I started stashing my own collection under my bed. I waited until everyone was asleep to admire them so no one would see me. Brooke, on the other hand, read them by the door every morning. She saw me watching one day, and I expected her to be embarrassed. Instead she held up the paper, smiling.

"This one is my favorite. It has the biggest picture."

"I like the photo of her running on the track," I admitted.

In my seventh-grade social studies class we talked about current events every Friday. While most kids brought in stories about Supreme Court decisions or local elections, I repeatedly discussed Jennifer's latest victory in cross-country. If anyone got sick of hearing about it I didn't notice. Every time she was in the paper, I signed up to present again.

Over the next few months Jennifer continued to run faster than anyone else in the region. In the weeks leading up to the state race her face appeared in the city papers again, this time next to a picture of Sara Gorton, a senior from another region with similar times. State was going to be a match race: Stirling v. Gorton.

On the morning of the race, we arrived early so Jennifer could warm up with her team. The freshly mowed park smelled of wet grass, and all around us were runners with bright uniforms and tight ponytails. Jennifer, like the others, was noticeably preoccupied that morning. The local hype over the long-distance face-off was taking its toll on her. Still, no one expected the extra attention would affect the outcome of the race. Jennifer was a driven winner by nature.

As the runners lined up, she looked down at her hands and turned to her coach, "My fingers won't stop tingling . . ."

"Take a few deep breaths," he said, "run your race, don't worry about anyone else."

He clapped her on the back and she jogged toward the lineup, her blond French braid bobbing up and down against her uniform. As she weaved slowly through the crowd of opponents I watched her face. It was expressionless, but her hands revealed what her eyes would not. Every few seconds she shook them in front of her body, closed them in fists, and clapped them together.

"Runners, on your mark!"

The announcer held a megaphone and a starter pistol.

"Get set!"

He lifted the gun above his head and a loud shot cracked through the air.

"Go," I whispered as the horde of runners burst forth into motion.

Earlier that morning Brooke and I had scouted out the course. We knew all the shortcuts around the park, and we had mapped out a plan to cheer Jennifer on in multiple spots throughout the race. The first time Jennifer passed she was in a group of ten runners in front. We yelled her name and ran down the hill and across the bridge to our next designated cheering location. A few minutes later she passed us again, going a little faster this time and alongside Sara Gorton. The next closest runner was at least two hundred yards behind them. Brooke and I high-fived and ran to our third destination, the two-thirds mark. Again, Jennifer and Sara were neck and neck, but this time the next runner wasn't even in sight. From there, the course went around a hill and wasn't visible again until the final stretch. We found a place near the finish and waited for our sister to come around the bend, in first place.

Several torturous minutes later we heard the crowd roar and saw Sara, not Jennifer, round the corner. *She'll be close*, I thought. *She can still pass her.* But Jennifer didn't come. Instead, there was a gap and then another girl ran into view, and another, and another. Brooke tugged at my shirt.

"Where is she?" she asked nervously.

I kept staring at the course. *No, this isn't right. Jennifer was going to win.* After a few agonizing minutes, Jennifer stumbled into view, and I knew something was terribly wrong. Brooke started to cry and tugged even harder at my clothes.

"What's wrong with her? Why does she look like that?"

I stared at Jennifer in disbelief—her face was the color of ash, her head tilted back, barely supported by her neck. Like a newborn animal trying to walk for the first time, her body shook with each step. I wanted to run to her, to hold her up and steady her steps, but doing so would disqualify her from the entire race. So I watched in shock as my famous sister staggered through the last hundred yards, disoriented, weak, and being passed on either side by girls who had never come close to her times. When she finally finished the race, I saw her collapse into the waiting arms of my father.

By the time Brooke and I got around all the ropes at the finish line, paramedics wearing neon-green vests had already surrounded our sister. One of them put an oxygen mask over her face while another stuck a needle in the crease of her arm. Blood squirted onto his sleeve, and he didn't even bother to wipe it off. My parents knelt on either side of her, so I held Brooke's hand and tried to be brave. We both sobbed while she went in and out of consciousness.

At the hospital the doctor explained that Jennifer had suffered a severe hyperventilation episode.

"The lack of carbon dioxide in your daughter's blood should have made her faint long before the finish," he told my mom.

But that's the thing about Jennifer: she didn't want to faint, she wanted to finish the race. Later that evening her coach stopped by to visit and deliver her medal. She got tenth place out of a couple hundred runners.

When the newspapers came out the next day a photo of Jennifer's fragile body covered the local sports section, side by side with a snapshot of Sara crossing the finish line. Jennifer cried and my mom gently threw them away. In her mind, she had failed her coach, her team, and herself. What she didn't realize was I had always secretly admired her, but that day of the race she became one of my heroes. I know how badly *I* wanted her to win, so I could tell my class that my sister was the best runner in the state; but watching her struggle to the finish after she had already lost was the most incredible thing I had ever seen. Later, I pulled a few articles out of the trash and took her medal to school for my current events presentation. I told my class about the race, what the doctor had said, and I passed her medal around the room.

"She could barely walk at the end, but she wouldn't give up until she crossed the finish line."

I had never been more proud.

SCARFMAN

My dad was practically born wearing a scarf and a hat. According to him, the Chicago winter of 1976 permanently damaged the nerves on the back of his neck, leaving him feeling eternally cold. He wears a scarf to work, to church, and all year round, even in Arizona. For as long as I can remember, he has only ever worn his scarves one way: hung limply around his neck. His straight-hanging scarf is a trademark, and from an early age I knew it set him apart from the other dads. In kindergarten, my class made cards for Father's Day and mine read, "I love my dad because he always wears a scarf and a hat, and it makes him easy to find at the beach." I should have also mentioned that it could double as a towel if needed.

Stephen J. Stirling is a sweetheart. But if my mom hadn't been around to clean his clothes and prepare his food, he'd still be sitting somewhere dressed in parachute pants, chewing on a piece of wood. My mom only went out of town once when we were kids. I remember, because my dad fed us cereal for breakfast, lunch, and dinner for three days in a row. Best three days of my life. Saturday was the one day he could sleep in, but every weekend without fail he woke up early to the sound of my little feet pitter-pattering toward his bedroom. I'd crack open the door, he'd crawl out of bed, and together we would have a cereal picnic on my blanky.

As a freelance screenwriter and journalist my dad was an exceptional storyteller. While we ate, he told me stories—both from his own life and the made-up lives he wrote about. He told me about the winter he started wearing scarves, which was after he opened an underground theater in Fresno, and right before he was chased out of the city by the Italian Mafia, who didn't want a theater there in the first place. He told me about the day he became an honorary member of the Black Panthers in high school, and the time he jumped through a window to get on the last train heading out of La Calera during the 1973 Chilean revolution. He told me about his post-college career as a vagabond, drifting around the country in an old camper. Along the way, he met Dick York from *Bewitched*, mayor Richard Daley of Chicago, Mormon leaders Gordon B. Hinckley and Thomas S. Monson, President Ronald Reagan, head of NASA Wernher von Braun, and Richard Simmons. He ended every story by reaching out his palm and saying solemnly, "And I shook his hand." I got more than a passion for cereal from my father; I inherited the desire to have a life full of adventures that I could tell stories about. And I wanted to shake everyone's hand along the way.

Once my sisters and I were born, my parents settled down and my dad sold his motor home. But he never did let go of his passion for life and adventure—even if the adventures changed from roaming the country to raising three little girls. When I was young he frequently worked from home in an office behind a set of glass-paned double doors. If the doors were closed, he was "at work," and we weren't supposed to go in. I always did anyway, but he never made me leave. I would lie on the ground with my blanky and listen to him type. The sound of a keyboard still makes me feel at home.

My dad's income as a writer was meager, to say the least. Even though I knew we weren't rich, I rarely felt poor as a child. Every weekend my dad searched the papers for free events, and sometimes he even pulled us out of school to attend. On the sign-out sheet he would write "Free day at the planetarium" in the column labeled REASON FOR LEAVING. Most frequently, these free events were city orchestra and symphony concerts, where I first saw and fell in love with the violin.

At six years old I wasn't a brilliant child, but I was smart enough to notice the important things—like the fact that the first chair violinist was always the star of the show, and that the violin section played the melody as well as the fastest parts, and was always seated toward the front of the stage. I had to get my little hands on one!

When I first brought it up, my parents were hesitant to invest in lessons. I was the child who played with a new toy for a few minutes and then moved right along to the next. But when I persisted my mom eventually started looking for a teacher. Most violin lessons were thirty minutes to an hour and anywhere from thirty to sixty dollars a session. At the time, my parents couldn't afford anything in that range. Instead of giving up, my mom searched until she found a college student who was willing to give me a fifteen-minute lesson every week for a low fee.

My first violin was made of cardboard—no bridge, no strings, no sound—just a cereal box with a paper towel roll attached to one end.

"This is your instrument for today," my teacher said with a smile.

I remember raising an eyebrow at my mom and thinking, *Oh no, she bought me cardboard box lessons.* But once I understood that the fake violin was temporary, I practiced holding it until I could do it with my eyes closed. When I demonstrated that I was coordinated enough to hold it correctly, I earned my first tiny violin.

For years my dedication to practicing annoyed Jennifer to no end, which is probably why I kept it up. "Mom, make her stop!"

she would yell. In return, I would squeak even louder. Shortly after I started, Jennifer picked up my dad's old trumpet. The mouthpiece was bent and permanently stuck to the body of the instrument so that it didn't fit in its case anymore. When Jennifer first expressed interest in playing the old horn, my dad tried to remove the mouthpiece with a pair of pliers and succeeded only in denting it further.

"It appears that this mouthpiece has severe separation anxiety. I think we better leave it where it is," he said.

He found an old briefcase that would hold it, and Jennifer carried her trumpet to and from school in that. It may have been misshapen, but Jennifer had no trouble making it work, and we were finally evenly matched. From that time forward, if she didn't want to listen to me practice, all she had to do was take out her trumpet and play even louder. When Jennifer had proven her devotion to the trumpet my parents got her a normal mouthpiece that fit inside a normal case. She excelled throughout high school and was the principal trumpet player in the band through college, where she majored in music performance. I take partial credit for her success. After all, it was I who motivated her—by being annoying—to practice so often as a child.

For the next five years my parents rented instruments from the local music store as I went through different sizes. When I was in the sixth grade I finally grew into a full-size violin. By this time I had proven I was dedicated to the instrument, and my parents decided to invest in a violin that could take me through high school. My music teacher had one for sale and my parents paid two thousand dollars for the violin, the bow, and the case. Two thousand dollars! The amount sounded crazy rolling off my tongue. I never told any of my friends how much my violin was worth, because I didn't think they would understand. To them it would be an expensive instrument, but to me it was the air-conditioning my mom's car didn't have and the unfinished floorboards in the basement.

Shortly after, my music teacher suggested I audition for a local orchestra called the Metropolitan Youth Symphony (also known as MYS to all the kids at school). By this time I was old enough to know that extra activities cost money, but when I was admitted into the second division group I was ecstatic. It was a bit of a stretch financially, but my parents made it work anyway.

At rehearsal every week my mom sat in the back of the room, clipping coupons and placing them in categorized Ziploc bags. One day she couldn't stay during rehearsal, so she sent my dad to pick me up. As I watched the other kids leave in their SUVs and sports cars, I saw my dad pull up in what my family referred to as "the Clunker"—a dented 1979 Buick Skylark with no AC and a ripped-up interior. My dad considered it a classic, but to me and everyone else it was rust on wheels. At that moment, it was smoking and rattling as he approached the curb. I considered ducking behind the nearest tree and walking home, but my dad leaned out the window and yelled, "Hey Lindsey, I need your help!" I dropped my head and walked quickly to where he was parked. He asked me to show him to the nearest water faucet—the radiator needed fluid. I was mortified. The only entrance to the bathroom was through the back of the rehearsal room, which was currently occupied by the first division symphony. I tried telling him there wasn't a bathroom nearby, but he insisted. So we pulled a few cups out of the trash and walked back and forth between the parking lot and the bathroom, collecting water for the Clunker. My face burned as we passed my peers, over and over, carrying water in filthy, dented cups. When we were finished, I sank in my seat and my dad cranked the engine until it finally started. The car roared and I felt the shame showing on my face—shame for the water in dirty cups, for the smoke coming from the Clunker's hood, for the sweat darkening the back of my dad's dress shirt. Looking back, I realize I should have felt shame for other reasons—like being embarrassed of a man who continued to drive a broken car so my sisters and I could go to our music lessons each week, and so that I could participate in a group like MYS.

As I got older, I started to notice my parents' quiet sacrifices more and more: the brown dress shoes my dad wore with black pants, the months my mom spent working in the high school cafeteria, the practical gifts they gave each other at Christmas, and the years we went without regular household appliances. When I was young, I thought my parents simply didn't care about having nice things. Now I know better. I wonder how many times they put new shoes, matching silverware, or working tools back on their wish list so we could continue to rent my violin, Brooke's cello, and Jennifer's trumpet. I'll never know, because they never drew attention to it. But last week, my violin performance got them into Disneyland for free, so I guess it all worked out okay.

Karma, she's not always as mean as they say.

JUNIOR HIGH, HIGH SCHOOL, AND OTHER PLACES

Only three things were important in junior high: wearing chunky skater shoes, fitting in, and getting noticed by Colby Brienholt. My friends and I nicknamed him the "Holy Hottie," and despite my long-suffering crush on the boy I never spoke more than ten words to him—five of which were, "Will you sign my yearbook?" He did sign it, and out of the goodness of his heart he asked me to do the same. I wrote "Call me" for the first time in my life, and (because this was before preteens had cell phones) I left my home phone number. It was also the first time I had ever made a move on a guy, and I felt empowered for the next hour or so. He never did call, and that landline got disconnected when my parents finally went cellular, so that ship has officially sailed.

I don't remember much else about junior high except that I learned several valuable lessons the uncomfortable way. For instance, boys were more interested in the girl wearing makeup and a push-up bra than the best-dressed cowgirl on Spirit Day. *But Johnny, I rubbed ash on my cheeks and wore genuine chaps!* I also learned that girls my age were shaving their armpits. I didn't have any armpit hair to shave at the time, so it never occurred to me that it was something I should be doing. Then one day on the bus ride to a cross-country race, Danielle Brown turned to me out of nowhere and said, "Hey, I'm trying to convince Chad that he should shave his armpits. Tell him how great it is."

My blank stare must have given me away.

"Don't you shave your armpits?" she asked casually.

She wasn't what I would call popular, but out of everyone on the cross-country team, she had the smallest nose and the loudest voice, making her the most desirable girl on the bus by default. At every cross-country event, she and the other situationally popular kids on the team sat together being loud. Somehow I was getting dragged into it. I remember sitting in silence for a moment, wondering which answer was the right one. I looked between Danielle and all the boys' faces for any clues before slowly answering, ". . . no." Her mouth fell open, and she gasped as if I had just told her I had a secret tail in my pants. Since my answer wasn't confident enough, she asked again, "You don't?"

I paused, debating whether or not I should change my answer, but the damage had already been done. I looked between her and Chad and said, "Well, umm . . . no, I don't."

She shrugged and turned back to her earlier conversation, leaving me to contemplate the absence of hair under my arms. That day I did terrible in my race because I was worried about lifting my elbows too far from my sides. When I got home I locked myself in the bathroom and used one of Jennifer's razors to shave. My armpits looked exactly the same as they did beforehand, but I felt like a new woman. At cross-country practice the next day, I placed both hands behind my head and walked extra close to Danielle so she would notice my smooth underarms. She took one look at me and said, "You should try using the liquid gel deodorant. It won't leave white smudges on your pits like you have there." Could. Not. Win.

Junior high was also when I noticed girls and boys were no longer regular friends. If a girl wanted to talk to a boy, she flirted. It was a foreign and terrifying language to me. I had always played sports and gotten along well with the boys in elementary school, but this was different. I didn't understand how I was supposed to interact with boys without acting like one. In the space of a few short months, I went from having the confidence of a swanky barnyard rooster to that of a field mouse. I didn't have a lot of friends, so I put my energy into things I could control, things I could practice. I was first chair violin in the orchestra, first chair flute in the band, and MVP of the soccer team. Outwardly, I had every reason to be confident, but I walked the halls quietly—careful not to say or do anything that might upset the delicate balance of the social scene. When I got to high school, I was still wearing fat skater shoes, but I slowly stopped second-guessing myself. Meeting "the girls" had everything to do with that.

We were friends by default, each of us searching for the least threatening lunch table on the first day of high school. I definitely wasn't going to take the seat next to Danielle Brown—who knew what other body parts I was supposed to be shaving?—so I sat down at an empty table in the back. As I opened my lunch, a girl with what I can only describe as fluffy brown hair approached one of the empty chairs.

"Hey, can I sit here?" she asked quietly, pointing to the seat across from me.

"Sure," I said, relieved that I wasn't sitting alone. "I'm Lindsey."

"Hey, I'm Michelle," she replied, taking a seat.

I recognized her as the girl who threw up at soccer tryouts in eighth grade, but I wasn't in any position to be picky. We must have looked harmless enough because soon after, two blondes approached the table.

"Are you saving these seats for someone?"

Michelle and I glanced at each other before shaking our heads in unison.

"Oh goodie! I'm Shelley, this is Amy," the shorter blonde said, pointing to the other.

She sat down like the table had been hers long before I arrived. Amy, the taller one, sat without a word, but Shelley grabbed her chair and continued to talk as if we were all old friends.

"Did you guys see the elderly lunch man at the sub sandwich register? He asked me if I wanted a box of 'mewlk' with my lunch. Cutest thing ever. I want to date him."

She took a bite of her sandwich and managed a closed-mouth smile as she chewed.

"So," she said after swallowing, "now that you all know my secret crush, who's yours?"

There was silence for a moment and then Michelle spoke with her mouth full.

"Oh, I got one. Harry Potter, from *The Goblet of Fire*." She swallowed forcefully. "When he escapes that dragon . . . Anyone?"

She looked around the table for approval. Shelley, Amy, and I looked cautiously back at her, trying to decipher if she was being serious or not. In the silence, Michelle laughed quietly at her own joke and looked down at her hands. In moments our collective awkwardness would spread over our table like mustard gas, so I jumped into the conversation.

"Oh yeah, Harry. He is so hot."

Immediately the smile returned to Michelle's face, and she nodded in agreement. To my left Shelley laughed freely.

Shelley was the kind of girl who you met and instantly wanted to follow around. She had a gravitating presence—not in an overbearing or controlling way, but more of a "Hey, I'm full of fun, exciting ideas and you could be part of it" kind of way. I *did* want to be part of it. When I returned the following day we made more awkward small talk about our classes and teachers. The awkward small talk turned into regular small talk, and then regular talk; and eventually, there was nothing regular about the way we talked at all.

Fast-forward a year and Michelle, Shelley, Amy, and I were still sitting together at lunch looking much the same, except Michelle's hair wasn't as fluffy and Amy wasn't as quiet. We were sophomores searching for adventure, so that year for spring break we decided to do something crazy. We loaded up the car with the essential snacks and set off on a road trip . . . to Sedona, Arizona, home of the National Cowboy Celebration and the KPC Peace Park. We stopped to look at some Native American dwellings, took a Jeep tour through

the desert, bought matching shirts at a gift shop—oh, were you expecting a story about wild drunken nights on the beach? I think you meant to buy Chelsea Handler's book. We did, however, take a picture on a bridge by a No Trespassing sign, so that was rebellious.

My friends and I didn't get into real trouble in high school. We got *real* into things like Spirit Week, school dances, and making music videos. When I turned sixteen I didn't get a car. Instead, I got RexEdit video editing software from my dad.

"Cool! What is it?" I asked carefully after I unwrapped the box.

"It's an editing program. You can make movies and stuff with it." He said the word *stuff* like the possibilities were endless. "No more stop-and-go on the camera."

This was before everyone had access to online editing programs, and our new software placed us on the cutting edge of technology. I was smitten—it was the coolest thing I'd ever seen! He showed me the basics and within days I had figured out how to do everything imaginable. At the time I wanted to be Avril Lavigne, so I convinced the girls to help me make a music video to "Sk8er Boi." This was still three years before the debut of YouTube (I feel so old) so when our project was finished, I put it on a videocassette (I feel even older!) and we proudly asked the student council to play it on the video announcements for our peers. For some reason, I didn't find our melodramatic performance at all embarrassing. On the contrary, I was quite proud of my lip-synching ability, and when it was finished, Shelley and I wasted no time in planning the next video shoot.

Eventually, we got so adept at making music videos that we decided to start producing our own movies, too. In fact, Shelley and I were so obsessed with filmmaking we convinced one of the production teachers to let us create our own video course during senior year. While everyone else in the class worked on a newsreel for the morning announcements, Shelley and I roamed the campus with a video camera making short films that were broadcast every

Tuesday. In our spare time, we took footage for the senior video. Our weekly videos ranged from Spirit Week commercials to random footage of us doing embarrassing things on campus. We were willing to do just about anything to get a few laughs, but sometimes our vision fell short and our classmates didn't respond to a video the way we'd planned. One particularly disappointing video was a short film we titled "Cornelius." Cornelius was a small red ball that we filmed rolling around campus making cute high-pitched *Weeee!* noises. Shelley and I assumed everyone would love Cornelius and that he would become a regular contributor to our videos. I had several episode titles in my head like "Cornelius Goes to Prom" or "Cornelius Joins the Pole Vault Team." Unfortunately, when "Cornelius Episode I" aired, I sank deep in my seat while my classmates stared blankly at the screen. Not a single giggle.

Every time one of our videos got a poor reaction, we became more determined than ever to make the next one so funny that everyone would have no choice but to laugh. The following week we made a short video called "Freshman Cam" where we zoomed in on unsuspecting and nervous-looking freshmen from afar. It was slightly insensitive, so naturally it was a huge hit.

That year we also came up with a feature-length film, "Elements," which we worked on tirelessly (sometimes even during "class"). It was a *Charlie's Angels* meets *X-Men* script, and we were convinced it was going to be a massive success. Since it was our biggest production to date, Shelley and I decided to hold auditions for the three available male roles. Because they were supportive, three of our closest guy friends showed up to read lines. Unfortunately, Justin and Heath were so terrible that we ended up giving all three roles to our friend Kyle, whose dream was to become a real actor someday. One of Kyle's characters was named Dr. Sullinoid, and to distinguish him from his other two roles, we made Dr. Sullinoid wear panty hose over his face. It was menacing and effective, not to mention much cheaper than hiring a special effects coordinator.

Once costuming was taken care of, we decided the opening scene was to take place in a lab, where Dr. Sullinoid kept evil potions and made villainous machinery. Since we didn't have access to a huge set, we settled for sneaking into a local community college to use one of the mechanical engineering rooms. How could we resist? All the machinery was perfect! We researched the schedule of courses, found out when the room would be vacant, and then simply borrowed it for a quick video shoot.

Another section of the film needed to take place at a crowded event, and since Shelley and I knew someone getting married that weekend, we jumped on the opportunity to film a few scenes at her wedding reception. I know, I know, it's horrifying, but keep in mind this movie was going to be a huge hit!

The production never did come full circle. After some searching, I found all the most important scenes on a cassette tape in my parents' basement. I recently watched it for the first time in years and I couldn't decide whether I was impressed or humiliated, but I was definitely entertained. And that's all that really matters in the end.

EVERYTHING IS
INAPPROPRIATE

Someone is always telling me to "slow down." Whether it's in reference to my driving, talking, or lifestyle, those two little words are constantly peeking over my shoulder. I humor them occasionally, but on the other shoulder is a conflicting voice that says, "You can slow down when you're dead, but today you need to go faster!" That voice also has a good point.

I've always lived in fast-forward, and as a child I practiced my violin incessantly until I could play whatever song I was working on at warp speed. It was exhilarating! My music teachers were constantly telling me to "slow down," so I did . . . at least during my lessons. But as soon as I was back to practicing, the race was on. I gained a few bad habits in the process (like my bent wrist) but I'm only human.

As the years passed I continued to play faster than I should have, but I improved in spite of it. Since my playing no longer annoyed Jennifer with the same gusto, I found new motivation to practice by joining the elementary school orchestra. I wanted to sit in that front chair, gosh darn it! Of course there were days when I would have preferred playing with Beanie Babies to playing Bach, but with some prodding from my mom I usually practiced anyway.

I was fond of sitting at the front of the orchestra for obvious reasons, and for years my progress fueled my desire to practice longer, harder, and faster. It was an energizing cycle. But when I got to high school I lost some of the fire and my ability plateaued. I still loved the violin and I was constantly making up my own music, but the classical pieces I played in school and for my lessons didn't hold my attention. Then one day I turned on my iPod and started jamming to Jimmy Eat World, and I couldn't stop. I didn't worry about my bow hand or the placement of my wrist; I listened to the music and played whatever came to my mind. I always knew I would never be one of the best classical violinists—because I didn't love classical music—but I have always loved the violin, and rock 'n' roll, and creating. When I put the three together, it felt like magic.

This was a few months into my sophomore year of high school. It was a more innocent time, when Chad Michael Murray was a total hottie and you were only as cool as the color of your Vans sneakers. Around this time Stomp on Melvin had a monopoly on the local garage band scene. They sang love songs, they wore skinny jeans—they were basically Greek gods but without the muscles. My friends and I were regular fangirls, and we attended every house party and show they played. But after a while I wanted to take a turn on the stage and tried to convince my friends to start a girl band. Our name was going to be Baked Fresh Daily and I had already written a few songs. Shelley usually humored my antics, but in this case she was the voice of reason.

"Great idea, Linds, except no one besides you knows how to play any instruments."

Shelley's brother was the drummer of Stomp on Melvin, so to get me off her back she finally asked him for a favor.

"Please let Lindsey jam with you at a few band practices. Please! If you don't, she's going to force me to play the bass guitar!"

Somehow, her brother agreed. That winter he invited me to play violin on one of their songs at a Battle of the Bands. As he put it, "Stomp on Melvin could use the extra edge." We got second place and the guys invited me to play a few more gigs. Then one day Randy—the skinny jean–wearing, smooth-talking lead singer—turned to me and said, "By the way, you're pretty much part of the band now." My stomach did somersaults but I played it cool and nodded.

One day during practice the lightbulb burnt out in the band room, and all the boys agreed I was the only one light enough to stand on the card table to replace it. I crawled up, Randy handed me the new bulb, and Adam stood by to steady the table. While I reached for the light I felt my shirt rise above my jeans, exposing my stomach. My belly was right about eye level with the boys, but I had pretty nice abs so I wasn't worried about it. I finished my job, lowered my arms, and jumped off the table like a nimble fawn. A few minutes later I went to the bathroom to wash my hands. Out of curiosity, I looked in the mirror and raised my arms. Instead of seeing an impressive stomach, I was mortified to find I was wearing my "last-resort underwear." I know you have them, too—a pair you keep around just in case you run out of clean "first choice" ones. Well, even if you don't, I had a few saggy, high-waisted Hanes I kept around for such emergencies. That day I was sporting a pair that sat at least three inches above my low-rise jeans, covering any hint of those "nice abs" I was so confident about.

No, no, no! You have got to be kidding me!

There was no way the boys hadn't noticed. What could be sexier than the puffy top of a pair of granny panties? I've been keeping the mystery alive since 1986. I pulled myself together, made up a quick excuse to leave, and went straight home where I burned all my last-resort undies—which was a behavior only slightly crazier than wearing them in the first place.

For the next several months I played every gig with Stomp on Melvin in front of a microphone. Although it increased my volume a little, I was still overpowered by all the electric guitars and crashing cymbals. After one of our first shows, my mom mentioned that she couldn't hear a single note I had played.

"It's almost like you don't need to be up there," she said.

"But I want to be up there," I replied, feeling discouraged.

Later, I brought up the idea of getting an electric violin, but it didn't take. However, after coming to several more shows and watching me play silently onstage, my mom's frustration got the best of her. She had, after all, paid for years of lessons—she wanted to hear me play.

We went to the music store where she found a Yamaha electric violin with a scratch, which we got at a discount. In the words of my mother, "What a gonga!" She says it means bargain, but it's really just a word she created to make secondhand shopping sound cool.

Another word that dominated my mom's vocabulary was *inappropriate*. It was the kiss of death from my parents, and their definition of the word was all encompassing. Being out past midnight— inappropriate. Using the words *shut up* or *fart*—inappropriate. Going camping with platonic guy friends—inappropriate. Wearing sandals to church—inappropriate.

When I asked my mom if I could go on tour with Stomp on Melvin that summer she didn't even pause.

"No, no. It's—"

"Mom, please, don't say it."

"Well it is, Lindsey. . . . It's *inappropriate*."

The word was acid to my ears. When my dad got home from work he looked sympathetic to my plea, but his response was equally disappointing.

"You're sixteen, you shouldn't be driving across the country with four older boys. Your mom is right—"

"No, Dad, don't—"

"It's *inappropriate*."

"Stop using that word!"

A few days later my parents came into my room and told me I could go on tour on one condition. I was elated. "Anything!"

"Your mom has to go with you."

Okay, I know I said "anything," but not a chance. I didn't even consider it. I never told the guys about the offer, but somehow they heard about it. And somehow, it was settled. My mom was coming on tour. I remember getting ready to leave and feeling so annoyed in that "Moms ruin everything" kind of way, but if my someday sixteen-year-old daughter were to ask me to go on the road with a few cute dudes, my answer would also be "Your mom has to go with you." My mom is the cat's pajamas—I just hadn't realized it yet.

In an attempt to give us a little space, she decided to drive separately behind Adam's old van. She told me to ride with the boys, but even my teenage self wasn't heartless enough to leave her alone in a car for eleven hours straight. I rode with her for a while until I felt like I had served my time. Then I jumped in the van with the boys and pretended my mom wasn't fifteen feet behind us, eating corn nuts and listening to *Harry Potter* on tape.

While I didn't exactly want my mom there, the guys loved having her around and affectionately addressed her as "Lindsey's mom." In the following weeks, she turned into quite the handy roadie. She helped us load and unload our gear, she frequently worked our small merch table, and she was helpful during sound check (almost always advising that "Lindsey needs to be louder"). We traveled through Arizona, Utah, and Idaho where the boys had connections, and every night we all crashed in someone's living room together.

"Good night, kiddos," she said.

"Good night, Lindsey's mom," they replied.

On top of being helpful as a roadie, my mom was also good at keeping away any unwanted guests. One night the guys invited some very attractive but highly annoying girls to hang out after the show. But once the ladies realized "Lindsey's mom" was going to be hanging out, too, the evening lost some of its appeal. I gave her a mental high five and realized having my mom around wasn't so bad after all.

Being in the band was a lot of fun, but I always knew it would be temporary. When the boys graduated and moved off in different directions, I missed the good old days. Still, at the time I had only a small crush on performing. It wasn't till a few years later that I really fell in love with it. It's one of the few moments in my life I can pinpoint down to the millisecond that it happened.

Every year my city puts on a Junior Miss Pageant in which senior girls can compete for scholarship money. I grew up watching friends and neighbors in my area participate, and when I was a senior in high school I couldn't wait to get on the stage. Like most pageants, this one judged us in the categories of academics, interview, poise, talent, and a cheesy (but surprisingly difficult) fitness routine in place of the swimsuit portion. *Don't forget to smile during those crunches!* But unlike most pageants, the focus of Junior Miss was to build confidence. For weeks, they worked with us—bringing in speakers and coaches who taught us how to walk, speak, and carry ourselves properly onstage. Luckily, being onstage didn't scare me. But when we started rehearsing the talent portion I became discouraged. There were several other violinists in the competition, one of whom had been first chair in the All-State Orchestra for the past two years. Skill v. Skill, I knew she was a better musician. But it wasn't only the violinists I was worried about. The pageant was full of amazingly talented girls who had fun and entertaining performances. There were Broadway singers, jazz dancers, and tumblers who had everyone smiling and clapping along in rehearsals. More than being a performer, I wanted to be an entertainer.

"I wish I had a talent that could show my personality, something that could get people smiling and cheering," I said to my mom one night.

"Well, why can't you do that with your violin?" she asked.

"No one is going to clap along with a classical solo."

"I guess you better not play a classical solo then" was her response.

In Stomp on Melvin, I had always played backup and simple harmonies, so it had never crossed my mind that the violin could be the lead in anything other than classical music. But my mom was right, why couldn't it be? We started brainstorming, and I decided I was going to write a rock song for the violin. After I wrote the melody, I asked a friend of a friend for help with the backtrack. We had never met, but he came to my house, set up a mobile "recording studio" in my basement, and recorded drums, bass, and guitar. Zac Beus, bless your soul. With my upbeat backtrack and rock melody in place, I now had to find a way to engage the audience and the judges. I needed to smile, move, and maybe even . . . dance.

Even when I was in a rock band, I never moved onstage. I didn't know how to be animated without losing my concentration, so I stood like a statue. Unfortunately, standing still and playing with a serious facial expression was not an option for this performance. Even more confusing than a rock violinist would be a rock violinist who didn't know how to rock.

You wouldn't believe the amount of concentration it took for me to smile while I played, let alone move my appendages independently of one another. In the following weeks I spent hours upon hours trying to pair basic movements with my playing—a step on the downbeat, a pop of the hip on the next, and a kick before the chorus. And my backbend? Unrecognizable. It was more like a back tilt—the backbend's clumsy baby sister. No matter, it did the trick. When I started my performance on opening night, the audience went wild. *A ~~dancing~~ moving violinist? Mind blown!* One of the judges raised his hands above his head and got the whole crowd clapping on the beat—more or less—but even if they had terrible rhythm, it was electrifying. When I finished the last note I was filled with the most incredible energy I had ever felt. As I looked out over the roaring crowd and the smiling judges I knew it had worked—I had them entertained. More important, I knew I had to chase this feeling. I ended up winning the talent portion, as well as the local and state titles as Junior Miss. A few months later I went to the national competition as Arizona's Junior Miss, where I performed on an even bigger, brighter stage—winning a sum total that put me through almost two years of college.

The scholarship money was a godsend for my family. But more valuable than the money was the moment of clarity after my performance, when I stood onstage as a solo artist for the very first time. I was head over heels.

My evolution as a violinist has included many thrilling performances, and I still love what I do, but there are times when even I get burned out. When this happens, I go back to that moment ten years ago. I picture myself on the stage with my bow in the air. I feel my heart racing, I see the faces in the audience smiling, and I remember the moment I thought, *I have to make this my life.*

THEY ARE
NOT ADOPTED

For a short time last year my brother lived in Georgia. When my tour passed through Atlanta, I put him with a plus-one on the guest list—at least I meant to. When the woman at will call told him (and his date) that he wasn't on the list, he insisted.

"I am her brother. Will you please look again? It is under Vladimir."

I should mention he looks nothing like me and has a thick Russian accent. His request sounded more like this:

"I am her braw-ther. Vill you please luke again, it is under Vladi-meer."

Meanwhile, in my dressing room, I heard a woman's voice coming through Erich's (my tour manager's) walkie-talkie.

"There's a foreign young man at will call, he claims to be the performer's brother . . ."

Erich looked at my apologetic face as he answered, "That's correct, please let him in."

The summer after my senior year of high school, my parents came into an unexpected inheritance. Before it even arrived my sisters and I had all but spent it in our minds. Jennifer could plan her dream wedding, I was going to be debt-free in college, and Brooke wanted a horse trailer. There would probably even be enough leftover cash to refinish the floor in the kitchen, get air-conditioning for my dad's car, and take my mom on that Alaskan cruise she had always dreamed of. Instead, my parents chose to spend the money on an adoption agency and three round-trips to Siberia. Typical Stephen and Diane. They were finished raising young children, so they decided to take on an even bigger challenge—two teenagers from Russia. There were a few complications with Marina's adoption, so Vova arrived first, two months shy of his sixteenth birthday. By this time, I was getting ready to leave for college out of state, so I spent as much time with him as possible.

I'd always imagined having a brother would entail living with a cool best friend who doubles as a yardman and sets up my tent on camping trips. Now, I just picture that monkey on YouTube that pees in his own mouth. A peeing monkey *that I love*, of course. One of the first things Vova did in America was roll down the back window and catcall (in Russian) at girls on the drive home from the airport. I was horrified. *Oh heck no, not* my *brother.* I tried explaining, "Noooo," shaking my head back and forth in the universal negative gesture, *Yelling is bad. Don't be that guy. Girls don't like that guy.*

He watched me pantomime about not being creepy for a minute then returned to the window to whistle at the next female we passed. *Really?* I thought. *But I just told you that was frowned upon.* I had spent most of my life wishing I had a cool brother, and he had spent most of his life trying to eat the food on his plate before someone stole it. I guess my expectations were a little high. Even if he wasn't quite prepared to be the well-mannered, protective brother I imagined, he turned out to be exactly the kind of brother I needed. The kind that makes fart noises every time I bend over.

Entertaining Vova was easy. He practically got off the plane dancing, and since he didn't speak English, dance was a language we could both understand. My friends loved taking him places, too (so long as the window lock was on), because he was outgoing, and on the dance floor it was near impossible to keep him from spinning in circles on his head. He was our party trick.

Connecting with Marina was a little more difficult. When she got to America I was already living in an eight-by-eight dorm room 650 miles away, and for a few years our relationship was limited to short holidays and family vacations. At first, these circumstances worked in my favor. While Brooke, Marina, and Vova struggled through the transition of re-creating the structure and dynamics of our nuclear family, I got to be the cool older sister who came home for a few days at a time and provided endless fun. We went shopping, got ice cream, and spent hours at the local ice-skating rink. Eventually, though, they navigated through the ups and downs of the new family dynamic at home, leaving me to be the disconnected older sister. I missed out on much of Marina's life, but during my short visits I learned a few key facts about her. She loved tumble-weeds, hated using the handheld translator to communicate, and didn't want anyone to know she was adopted.

When Marina first expressed that she didn't want us to use "the A word," it was understandable. But avoiding the topic was some-times (always) a challenge.

Accents are a huge conversation starter. All day long, cashiers, clerks, waitresses, receptionists, bag boys, and the guys behind the ticket counter followed the same script.

"How are you today?"

[Generic response here.]

"Great."

Then a beautiful teenager with exotic looks and an accent like warm honey walks up and *BAM*, new topic of conversation!

The exchange usually went as follows:

"I love her accent, where is she from?"

When we said "Russia," the follow-up question was always the same.

"Oh, is she a foreign exchange student?"

I'm going to remind you—Marina didn't like it when we told people she was adopted. I agree with her, the word *adopted* is quite disjointed. I think it is the sound of the "p" next to the "t" that makes it so abrupt. Or perhaps she didn't want complete strangers knowing personal details about her life for the sake of small talk. It made sense, but going places with her was like playing the board game Taboo: *Explain the origin of your Russian sister without using the word* adopted.

When the foreign exchange student question surfaced, my mom would smile and say, "No, she's my daughter." Without fail, the person asking the question would pause, the gears turning in their head. *But how can she be your daughter when she is clearly from another country?* When my mom didn't offer an explanation, they often asked, "Is she adopted?"

My mom would smile and reply again, "She's my daughter."

At first, these interactions were painfully awkward—watching my mom dance around the question, usually asked by some teen employee who was simply trying to engage with the customer. But in the grand scheme of things, it was a simple gesture. I've always appreciated a good game of Taboo.

After my sophomore year of college, I took a year and a half off of school to be a missionary for my church in New York. When my mission ended, I had a few months to kill before the new semester started at Brigham Young University. In the interim, I moved back home to Arizona for a few months. Marina was attending the community college, and for the first time since she had ~~been adopted~~ come to America, we were living under the same roof. This time, I was the one reacclimating to normal life, and she took me shopping, out for ice cream, and to see all the movies I had missed over the last year and a half. Around that time I had started dating a guy who was perhaps too much of a gentleman. I wanted him to kiss me, but he wasn't making any moves. One night, Marina and I ended up at the park in our pajamas with a gallon of Blue Bell ice cream and two disposable spoons. Between bites I expressed my frustration.

"He's just not getting the hint."

"Com'on, make him kiss you" was her reply.

"I haven't kissed a boy in years. I don't remember how!"

Marina had always been a bit of a mythical creature. Unlike me, she knew how to balance innocence with opportunity.

"Okay, okay," she said. "At the end of the night when he drops you off, hug him. Let it linger a little, but not too long, and then pull your head back, but leave your arms around him."

She held up her spoon and gazed at it.

"Look in his eyes, then look at his lips, and the magic will happen."

A few nights later, when I got home from my date, I woke her up.

"Pst!" I whispered. "I made the magic happen!"

She lifted her head slowly from the bed. "Get over here and tell me all about it, you little slut," she whispered back.

Since the day my family decided to adopt (I don't know how else to say it!), I felt like her sister. I always knew I wanted to be there for her and build a friendship that could last a lifetime. But that night was the first time she felt like *my* sister.

I know my relationship with Marina and Vova wasn't formed under ideal circumstances, and sometimes I feel like I've been cheated. I missed their entire childhood, and I never got to manipulate them into doing my chores. I was in college and on my mission for most of their teenage years, and now we're adults living separate lives on different sides of the country. For years I worried I might never have a close relationship with them, but I've since learned that love and family can trump time and circumstance. I love you, Vovi. And you too, Marini—you little slut.

TWO

THE "I WANT TO MAKE IT SO BAD I'LL SELL MY SOUL" PART, MIXED WITH A LITTLE "WHY DO I KEEP FAILING?"

If for a while the harder you try, the harder it gets, take heart. So it has been with the best people who ever lived.

—JEFFREY R. HOLLAND

SISTER STIRLING

I never planned on serving a mission for my church[1], it just sort of happened. In fact, when it came down to it, I never fully admitted I was going to go. In the months leading up to my departure, I responded to questions by saying I was "considering it" until, suddenly, I was standing in the Missionary Training Center and a little old lady was pinning a name tag on my blouse. Despite my previous

---

1 The Church of Jesus Christ of Latter-day Saints, to be exact. Since that is a mouthful, some people simply say the LDS, or Mormon, church. Cue influx of both fan mail and hate mail.

reservations about leaving my home to preach the good word, it felt like the only place I should be at the time. I also thought serving people for a year and a half would make me a better, happier person. I was being selfishly selfless.

Selfishly selfless: Selfless behavior resulting in positive recognition for good deeds, warming the heart and causing feelings of being noble and heroic.

When I got assigned to New York, I was ecstatic. I had always wanted to live in a big city, and this was *the* big city. Much to my dismay, after going through six weeks of missionary training, I was sent to Kingston—a tiny rural area upstate, where trees are taller than buildings and bugs are regular dinner guests. I had anticipated hailing taxis, riding busy subways, and proselytizing the masses on the bustling streets of the Big Apple. Instead, I spent my first night in a log cabin, nestled deep in the woods near Catskill Park. Within hours of my arrival, my companion (the official term for my missionary partner) took me to eat dinner with a family from the congregation. I sat in a disappointed daze as Brother Silas plucked a fat tick from the family cat right before my eyes.

"Uh oh, Copernicus has ticks again," he observed nonchalantly, handing it to his wife right over the stew we were about to eat.

"Would you look at that, it's a big one this time," she responded, looking over the bloodsucker between her fingers. She gave it a good squeeze and then washed it down the sink, returning once more to preparing our food.

I'll be honest, I wanted out.

Being a missionary in Kingston was challenging for a number of reasons. I guess I should say being a missionary in general was challenging for a number of reasons. Mostly because it was nothing like I expected. I had imagined myself doing good deeds and feeling fantastic about it. If I had enough faith, life-changing experiences would fall into my lap, right? For weeks I worked hard, waiting for the huge emotional payoff (selfishly selfless again). But instead of finding fulfillment, I faced one disappointment after the other. No one wanted to listen to my message, and after three months as a missionary, I hadn't changed a single life. This continued until I decided the first life I needed to change was my own.

I wish I could say the shift in my attitude brought me immediate success, but it didn't. In fact, shortly after this adjustment, someone spit a loogie on me. I dry-heaved for a solid minute. But it was okay, because by this time I no longer felt entitled to grandiose blessings. I could have gone without someone's phlegm on my shoulder, but I survived. That's when I learned what it felt like to be selflessly selfless.

Selflessly selfless: Selfless behavior resulting in negative recognition, or no recognition at all.

I'll let you in on a little secret: being selflessly selfless was really hard for me. By this point in the book, it should come as no surprise that I crave attention. I love a good pat on the back more than my neighbor's fifteen-year-old dog. Learning how to put other people's needs before my own was not easy, but at least I can say I tried.

When I was finally transferred to Manhattan, I was determined to make a fresh start. At first I saw everything as a gift. The honking taxis were music to my ears, the smell of housing projects was urban perfume, and the profanity of people on the streets was a colorful local dialect. Unfortunately, the novelty of the city soon wore off as my new companion and I struggled to find anyone to teach. *Let me tell you about Jesus, gosh darn it!*

Frequently, we stood on street corners trying to make contact with people as they walked by. Most either ignored us or stopped just long enough to say something offensive. After a discouraging morning, I approached a man who fired a string of curses and insults long enough that if you laid them end-to-end, they might stretch around the entire island of Manhattan. As he walked away I leaned against a building where I could cry without my companion noticing. It was a busy afternoon, and I disappeared easily into the crowd. For several seconds, I stood there sniffling into my scarf. Then, from behind I heard a slow, warm voice.

"Oh honey, are you far from home?"

I turned to see an African-American woman pushing a stroller. Her hair was wrapped in a traditional-looking headscarf, and she had a rich Caribbean accent.

I wiped my eyes quickly and replied, "Yes."

She put her hand on my back and spoke gently, "God loves you, and He knows you. That will give you strength."

Then she wrapped her arms around me and gave me a big hug. It was a simple gesture—a few kind words and a hug from a stranger—but it was everything to me that day. There I was, trying so hard to help other people, and someone ended up helping me. Look at me, I'm blubbering. Now get out there and hug a stranger today. But don't be weird or creepy about it. And if they ask you to stop, you should respect that.

When I wasn't getting yelled at or hugged on the streets, I was most likely riding the subway or a local bus. At the beginning of my mission, finding a seat on the subway was a gift from God. Given the opportunity, I would melt into my chair, close my eyes, and take a very literal load off my two aching feet. But as time passed, I became so discouraged that the only thing I could think to do was give up entirely, or work even harder. The latter meant no sitting. I started purposely standing so I could stay awake and talk to the people en route. Even if no one would let me into their home to teach them, they couldn't stop me from talking to them on the subway.

One day, I noticed a handsome gentleman standing to my right. He was tall, blond, and had tattoos running up and down both arms. More than anything else, I was compelled by the sadness in his eyes. Without much thought I asked him if he was okay. His eyes drifted up from the floor and when he realized I was talking to him, he responded, "Oh, yes . . . Just work."

"Rough day?" I asked.

To my surprise he began talking openly.

"Yeah, I guess. I'm just not happy with my job . . . it's not what I want to be doing, and I hate where my life is headed." He looked back down at the dirty subway floor. "I just don't have a purpose anymore." He paused as if he was going to continue and then looked back at me sheepishly. "Oh, I'm sorry, you probably don't want to hear that."

I smiled and reassured him, "Trust me, I wouldn't have asked if I didn't want to know. So what is it you do for work?"

He mumbled something that sounded like "escrow."

"I'm sure there's good business for that around here!" I replied.

He looked at me curiously, but didn't elaborate. Instead, he asked me about my line of work, which is when I pointed to my name tag and said happily, "Sister Stirling."

Immediately his pupils doubled in size, and he began apologizing profusely.

"Oh my gosh I am *so* sorry, I did not know you were a nun!"

His reaction caught me by surprise, but I assured him I was neither a nun nor offended. By this time my stop was approaching and I knew my chances of seeing him again were slim, so I didn't mind coming off strong. Without pausing to think about it I told him God *did* have a purpose for him, and that God was aware of his needs. The subway car was slowing so I finished quickly.

"I know this might not be the reassurance you were hoping for, but I would love to send some of my friends to talk with you about our church, if you're interested."

He paused and to my surprise said, "Sure. I would like that."

The subway stopped, he handed me a business card, and I

stepped out onto the platform. As the doors closed behind me, I looked down at the card. His name was Michael, but his title didn't involve the word *escrow*. It said MALE ESCORT. I had just congratulated a prostitute on his booming business . . . Since his address was out of my assigned area, I passed his information on to another pair of missionaries. I never saw Michael again, but at the end of my mission another missionary approached me at a conference.

"Hey, you're Sister Stirling, right?"

"Yes, that's me."

"Do you remember speaking with a man named Mike on the subway a while ago? Very tall, lots of tattoos."

"Yes! How could I forget?" I replied.

"I'm one of the missionaries who ended up with his contact information. He's been taking the lessons for almost a year, and last month he got baptized. We set him up with a new job now, too."

I was nearly speechless.

"But how did you know I was the one who passed on his information?" I asked.

"Whenever anyone asks him how he found the church, Mike talks about you. Says he met a little short-haired angel on the subway."

I was very humbled by it all, but it also felt incredible. Service is often like that. No matter how badly we want to believe we are doing it for the greater good, deep down we also know it's a personal tactic to boost morale and reduce stress pimples. But the truth of the matter is this: when I met Mike, I was in the dumps. In fact, I'm pretty sure I thought I was the biggest missionary failure on the planet—no, in the *history* of the planet. Come to find out, I did make a difference in someone's life, and he called me an angel. (If I were selflessly selfless, I probably wouldn't have shared that story, but as I told you, this is really hard for me. To prove I can be selflessly selfless, I *won't* tell you about the time I saved a baby who was stuck on a runaway horse in Central Park. Don't ask me how it got on the horse in the first place; that part's not important.)

Sister Buhler and me before street contacting.

Sister Buhler and me after street contacting.

I'm not going to sugarcoat it. Being a missionary is hard with a capital H, and during the eighteen months that I served, I was spit on, pushed, yelled at, and called a number of insults I didn't yet know existed. *Who you calling dingleberry, buddy!* I spent hours chasing people down in subzero temperatures and told complete strangers that Jesus had a plan for them. Now, I know what you're thinking: *being a missionary sounds like a terrible experience.* Hold on, I'm not finished yet! On the flip side, it was a magical time when my life was stripped of distractions, and I knew exactly what was important. I had a clear purpose, and even the smallest gestures became sublime—like teaching a teenage boy how to pray for the first time. It was a simple, beautiful time that I wouldn't trade for anything.

I get asked about my religion all the time. People want to know if I am a Mormon because I was born into it, or if it is still something I actively believe in today. I feel like this is a valid question.

When I was a kid, Sunday was a day for worship and family. We didn't travel, work, play with friends, watch movies, or listen to non-gospel radio. We went to church for three hours, spent time together, and danced to classical music as a last resort for entertainment. For years, I lived under the umbrella of my parents' faith because I trusted them, but my mission forced me to find strength in my own testimony.

In the music industry I get a lot of public judgment. Any time the topic of my religion surfaces, there are always people who react negatively, telling me to leave my crazy beliefs out of it. The problem is, I can't. My beliefs are as much a part of my being as my music, or my family, or my obsession with earthy-tasting cereal. Luckily, after all the rejection I faced on my mission, I'm no longer afraid of negative reactions. I've already heard it all—face-to-face. Hateful comments still hurt, but they don't hold the same weight they once did. Besides, say what you want, but I'm a short-haired angel. (Or at least I was to one man on a subway.)

TIPS FOR FUTURE
MISSIONARIES, NUNS, OR JEHOVAH'S WITNESSES

1 If you're trying to talk with people on the street, don't make eye contact until the last second. It's a lot like catching a chicken. One sudden move and they're off and running.

2 Always check to see if your dress is tucked into your panty hose before leaving the apartment, or any bathroom. It's hard enough to be taken seriously as it is, without your butt being exposed.

3 Skipping lunch breaks in order to work harder does not equal more success; it makes you seem tired and crazy. (I'm sorry I made you skip lunches, Sister Johansen.)

4 If someone takes your number rather than giving you theirs, hate to break it to you, but they're never going to call. Bonus: You can apply this tip to dating, too.

5 If people are mean to you, the best response is to nod and walk away. Turning the other cheek was always hard for me, but yelling, "How do you sleep at night?!" never made the situation any better.

6 If you hate it a little bit and wish you could go home when things get hard, you're not a bad person, you're a normal person. Just try not to dwell on it.

7 Your grandmother and her grandmother before her were right about shoes: comfort over fashion. Who are you trying to impress, anyway? Keep walking, and try not to look down at the boats on your feet.

8 If the rulebook says "Lights out at 10:30" (and it does), then buy a candle. You'd be surprised how easy it is to play Go Fish by candlelight.

I LOVE THE STAGE,
IT LEARNED
TO LOVE ME

I think college is a lot like childbirth. I've never pushed a baby out myself, but I hear it's comparable to doing squats over a pile of flaming swords. Even after that remarkable sensation, mothers all over the world go back for more. It's not that they don't remember the flaming swords; they just choose to focus on the more rewarding aspects of the experience. When I think about college I remember drinking powdered milk to save money, donating plasma to make money, and sleeping in a bunk bed I worried might collapse on top of me every night. But squatting and flaming swords aside, I loved college. Or at least I love the memory of college now.

Prior to my mission I spent two years at Brigham Young University. When I returned to school in the fall of 2009 most of my former roommates had moved on, but Brooke was now attending BYU as well. We moved into the cheapest apartment we could find with four other girls, and spent the next two years sharing a small room at the end of the hallway. In fact, with the exception of boys and deodorant, Brooke and I shared everything—a bunk bed, clothes, groceries, a sense of humor, powdered milk, and a car. Close quarters or not, we were usually together by choice. If one of us got invited to a party, we both went. If one of us wanted a midnight snack, we both ate. If one of us accidentally threw away the other's birthday present along with the wrapping paper, we both climbed into the dumpster to look for it. And when we weren't dumpster diving, we spent a large portion of our time at local venues. It was refreshing to hear new music, and I performed whenever possible.

Brooke and me sharing the experience of
wearing spandex onesies to a football game.

Before I left for New York, I started experimenting with the idea of playing violin to hip-hop tracks and dancing simultaneously. I made a short routine to the song "Pump It" by the Black Eyed Peas and put it up on YouTube, which was still new. My family watched it, Jennifer shared it with all her college friends, and I sent it to Ellen DeGeneres in hopes of being "discovered." She'd had cup stackers on her show, for heaven's sake. I didn't have a big ego, but I was certain I could out-perform a kid with some plastic cups. Several months passed, and I didn't hear anything back, so I put my dancing violinist dreams on hold and left on a mission. When I returned home, I was eager to lose myself in the hullabaloo of college life and music once again.

As a dancing violinist I wasn't exactly in high demand. To make myself known, I started going to every open mic night I could find in Provo. When it was my turn to perform, I'd hand my iPod to the man in the sound booth and instruct him to "just press play" on one of my hip-hop tracks. Then I'd walk confidently to the four-by-four stage and try not to fall off as I danced my heart out for the next eight minutes. It's hard to explain what it was like playing to a backtrack, on a stage alone, in front of a few people, in a dimly lit room. I used to think a smaller show meant less pressure. I soon learned that the smaller crowds were the hardest to entertain. There is less energy in the room, and it's altogether too easy to make awkward eye contact with every person in the audience. I always felt a little out of place at these events—breaking up the rhythm of the night's lonely guitar ballads with my electronic set—but every now and again, one solitary woman signed up to read poetry, and I didn't feel so alone. Although her microphone time did little to increase the energy in the room, it certainly made me feel like I had an accomplice. *You read your poetry slowly, I'll dance around the stage quickly, and we can share responsibility for the deeply uncomfortable feeling in the room afterward.*

Doing these performances was never my favorite thing, but I went back time after time because I didn't know where else to go. At the end of my music set each week, I would stop dancing and the confused crowd would clap politely. Then Brooke would let out a single loud cheer and we'd call it a night. Better luck next time.

Another method of publicity I used was the shameless self-introduction. Whenever I heard a band I liked, I would eagerly seek them out, introduce myself, and volunteer my services if they "ever needed a violinist." We would exchange phone numbers, and with few exceptions, people rarely took me up on my offer. Regardless, I threw myself into any opportunity I could find to play in front of a crowd. I played at parties, talent shows, weddings, and of course mic night after mic night after mic night.

In my attempts to take advantage of every opportunity, the opportunities started taking advantage of me. One night I had a negative experience playing with a local group, and on the drive home Brooke became my self-declared manager.

"That was ridiculous. What a waste of your time and talent. From now on, all your gigs go through me," she said.

Here are a few typical conversations with Manager Brooke:

"Lindsey, you didn't get paid enough for that open mic night last week. You killed it!"

"That's because I have to pay them to perform."

"Get them on the phone—*NOW*."

Or, "Hey Lindsey, I got you a gig at a retirement home. You got the one o'clock bingo slot."

"No you didn't."

"I know, but wouldn't that be fun?"

Even if Brooke was a terrible "manager," she did come to almost every performance I played. When I politely told her she didn't have to attend, she replied: "I'm your manager, of course I have to come. What if someone tries to book a show, and I'm not there with my planner?"

A few months later I was hired to play at a neighborhood block party. Brooke accompanied me, eager for a change of scenery and some free food. Little did we know, we were stepping into the block party event of the century.

When I was a kid, a block party meant Crock-Pots in a cul-de-sac, but this was a full-blown carnival. There were bouncy houses, a dunk tank, water slides, a face-painting station, a balloon man, and—that's right—a dancing hip-hop violinist. The man who hired me, who was the mastermind behind the whole party, had a schedule of events hung across his garage door. In the column for 7:00 P.M. it read, "Performance by Hip-Hop Violinist Lindsey Stirling," and in the adjacent column for 7:30, it said, "Candy Cannon."

"That sounds intense," I said, pointing out the cannon to Brooke. She nodded in approval, her mouth full of complimentary chips. "Oh yeah, we can't miss that."

An hour later I finished playing my set, and the host of the block party handed me a check.

As if he were speaking to several hundred people, he belted to the small crowd, "Thank you, Lindsey! That was fantastic. Next on the schedule is the candy cannon. Everyone gather 'round!"

Gingerly, he placed a wooden canister on the lawn.

"This is my first attempt at a cannon," he said. "I hope it works. Everyone stand back until it goes off!"

He lit a small wick at the bottom and stepped to the side. Everyone waited patiently for candy to come popping out of the top, but instead there was a pause, followed by an enormous *BOOM!* The entire thing exploded, spewing burning chunks of wood and candy into the air. For a split second, children and adults gazed up at the candy in delight, watching it rise higher and higher. Then the realization hit: everything going up—candy, shrapnel, and fire—would immediately be coming back down. Parents scrambled to grab their children, everyone ran for cover, and Brooke and I crouched behind a nearby car as smoldering candy rained from the sky around us. One particularly large piece of wood landed on a truck to our left and the alarm started blaring. Brooke looked at me, her eyes wide with a mixture of fear and pure joy.

"This guy is nuts! I heard him say this is an annual party. Put it on your calendar, we're coming back next year."

We never did make it back to the block party, but a few months later I landed another solo gig at a water park. I found out about a summer social for college students in Provo, and I tracked down the woman in charge of entertainment. I casually offered (begged) to play, and to my surprise, it worked! I got the opening slot right before another no-name band, some dudes who called themselves Imagine Dragons. After I finished my short set, Brooke and I spent the remainder of the evening going up and down the vortex slide with a new spring in our step. A real gig and free admission to a water park on a Tuesday? Life was good.

Given the opportunity, I might have happily played at block parties and water parks indefinitely. Unfortunately, these types of performance prospects were few, so I returned to the open mic night routine. This is where I eventually chanced upon a group called The Vibrant Sound. The first time I heard them perform, I was mesmerized. I had never heard anything quite like it—but more than that, they had a charisma and vitality onstage that was unparalleled. As Brooke and I left at the end of the night, the lead singer stopped me on my way out of the venue.

"Hey, you played the violin tonight," he said.

"Yeah, that was me."

"I'm McKay Stevens."

He held out his hand and I shook it.

"I'm Lindsey."

He was bald but attractive, confident but not overbearing.

"Man, I love your style," he said, still gripping my hand. "We could really use some of your sound. You have to come play with us sometime."

We did the phone number exchange and a few days later McKay actually called, inviting me to one of their band practices.

For the next few years, I shared the stage regularly with The Vibrant Sound, both as a guest performer and a solo artist. I recognized in them the passion and energy I craved in my own music. I could go on and on about McKay as a person and a musician, but I'll settle for saying he was one of my first inspirations in the music community and became a friend who is more like family. A few years later, when I started my first world tour, I asked McKay if he would come as my opening act. I wish I could say I did it to return the favor, but in reality I loved his music and wanted to bring someone I could trust. My motives were selfish, but I'm not apologizing.

DISORDERED
EATING

Up to this point, most of the book has been full of sunshine and rainbows, because let's face it, I grew up well. Good parents, good friends, good neighbors, good schools, good opportunities. But we all have *something*. I don't want to draw too much attention to my something, because it's not a badge of honor. I'm not proud of it, and I don't feel like a stronger or better person for having gone through it. On the contrary, it rendered me weak and crippled for years, and it cost me much more than I ever gained. It's a part of my past, not a part of who I essentially am as a person. If we're clear on that, I'll share my struggle in the hopes that some of you may become stronger and quicker to face and overcome your own "somethings," whatever they may be. So here it is: I had an eating disorder.

The first time I admitted it, the words burned in my throat, like I was swallowing coals. Even now I don't like the sound. When people hear the word *anorexic*, they automatically associate it with starvation and skipping meals, but those are merely the symptoms of a much bigger mental battle.

For as long as I can remember, I have been hyperaware of my size: the curve of my hips, the roundness in my face. Like talking out of turn or playing the violin, I always wanted my thin waistline to be one of my defining characteristics.

When I was eight, my family took our first trip to the snow. I remember putting on a gray snowsuit and staring at my reflection in the hall mirror, pinching and pulling at the sides of it, trying to find my waistline beneath the puffy polyester. It was the color of dust and the extra material engulfed my body, causing me to look large and feel insignificant. I found a belt, wrapped it around my midsection, and tightened it to define my waist again. I didn't do this to impress boys or my friends—I was eight. I did it for myself. I did it because somewhere beneath my skin lingered a subtle self-consciousness, planted by who knows what. And that's as far back as I can trace it.

Insecurities aside, I have always been petite. But in high school it bothered me that my jeans hung limp on Brooke's body. Brooke loved wearing my clothes but routinely complained about not filling out my jeans properly. She wanted to be curvier like me, and I wanted to be smaller like her. For a while that's all it was—a desire to look a little different—but by the time I entered college, I was plagued with fear of the "freshman fifteen." I was rooming with Michelle, and she had to count calories for a Sports Nutrition class. Since we ate almost every meal together, I too started consuming my food by the numbers. I knew the appropriate caloric intake for a girl of my age and level of physical activity was about two thousand calories a day, but I was never satisfied with meeting the quota. I always had to be well below: 1,600, 1,400, 1,200 . . .

Later, this habit trickled over into my mission in New York, a place overrun by freshly baked goods and greasy street food. Everywhere I went, people were telling me what I "just *had* to try" next.

"Have you tried Magnolia Bakery? The banana pudding is to die for."

"You must go to John's Pizzeria while you're here!"

"The Bagel Hole has the best honey cream cheese I have ever tasted."

The list of decadent must-haves went on and on. So, in addition to walking around New York City all day every day, I cut back on my overall food intake even more to compensate for these occasional indulgences. A bagel for breakfast meant skipping lunch, and dessert at night meant smaller meals the next day. It was a careful balancing act, and when I failed to comply, I felt physically and emotionally heavier as a result. In my mind, I "ate carefully" and lost weight "casually." My mom, of course, noticed.

Dear Lindsey,

You look so thin in your pictures. They say the camera adds ten pounds, but you look smaller than ever. Are you eating enough? I'm so proud of you, but don't work yourself to death, please. . . .

Dear Mammy,

Don't worry, we have plenty of food, but I'm also working hard and staying busy. Chasing after people in the name of Jesus is hard work. It's the sinners who run away the fastest! Just kidding, but there is no need to worry. . . .

I honestly didn't think there was any cause for concern. So what if I avoided greasy foods and ate copious amounts of veggies? Isn't that every mother's dream?

It wasn't until I got back from New York that my "healthy" habits spun out of control, and I lost the ability to discern between healthy and unhealthy thoughts. It wasn't only an issue at mealtimes; my eating disorder completely engulfed my life, dictating what I ate, my emotions, and how I saw myself in the mirror. Still, I continued on with my life, all the while thinking my thoughts were normal. It's hard to recognize a problem that is gradually consuming your mind.

For a while, my surroundings made it easy to ignore the problem. I was a junior in college, living with Brooke, and our other roommates were straight out of a sitcom. We were six peas in a very small pod. Cassie was the glue of our group and every night, like moths to a flame, anyone home would congregate in her room to avoid doing more pressing things (like homework or getting sleep). Frequently, these late-night gatherings involved watching consecutive episodes of ABC's *The Bachelor* on Cassie's old-school computer monitor. She had graduated the year before and worked as a social worker at a corrective school for teenage girls. After a long day at work, I suspect she enjoyed watching the train-wreck scenarios, because for once she didn't have the added responsibility of fixing them.

One night, after a particularly entertaining and heart-wrenching episode, our roommate Kelsey entered the room wearing a black leotard and high heels.

"What do you guys think?" she asked, posing dramatically against the doorframe. "For the church talent show. I'm thinking of performing the dance from Beyoncé's 'Ego' music video, but I'd need two of you to back me up."

She looked between Cassie, Brooke, and me as she slid clumsily into the splits, snagging one of her heels on the old carpet.

"Oh my gosh . . . You can't be serious. Do you know the dance already?" Cassie asked.

Kelsey answered with a grin. "What do you think I've been doing for the last three hours? Studying?"

"Show us, now!" Cassie yelled.

Kelsey pulled up a chair and started dancing.

Immediately, Brooke and Cassie succumbed to uncontrollable laughter. I knew it was funny, but my laugh felt unnatural. Usually these moments pulled me away from my thoughts, but more and more I felt myself getting sucked back in by something more powerful than my desire to be involved. When Brooke finally caught her breath, she got off the floor and started to dance behind Kelsey.

"I'll do it, but I will *not* wear a leotard," she said.

Kelsey waved her hand back and forth, "Fine, fine, fine."

Brooke reached out her hand, pulling me to my feet.

"I need backup!" she yelled.

I danced for a minute before sitting back on the floor. I felt like I was in a cage, watching, but unable to experience anything for myself. Something inside me had gone missing. I couldn't see it, but I could feel it. Cassie's laugh startled me out of my thoughts and I looked up to see Kelsey awkwardly sliding off a rolling office chair.

"Gosh darn it! Not even Beyoncé could do this dance on wheels," she protested.

"Maybe if you took off your heels—" Brooke suggested.

"Never!" Kelsey yelled back, sliding off the chair completely.

Her backside hit the floor first, sending her legs above her head. One heel caught on Cassie's desk, sending its disorganized contents crashing to the floor. This time my laugh came naturally and I gave myself to it freely, momentarily escaping my preoccupations.

Aside from the laughter in Cassie's room, I felt the most content after a long run or a small meal, so I ran longer, and I ate smaller.

Other than my shrinking appetite I was still leading a relatively normal college life. One afternoon in February, Brooke arrived home early from class and caught me as I was pouring a bowl of cereal.

"Stop!" she yelled. "Did you know it's Susan B. Anthony's birthday?"

I stared back and said, "I love Susan B. Anthony . . ."

"Yeah, me too. We should probably celebrate."

"Wanna go to Guru's?" I asked.

It was our favorite restaurant and the only place we went to celebrate "special" occasions.

"Uh, yes." She said it as though the answer was obvious.

Ten minutes later we were seated in a corner of the restaurant and ordering the usual, a cilantro-lime quesadilla to share.

"Ooh look, I see a first date at four o'clock," I said, gesturing to a couple seated across the room. "I'll be the boy this time."

It was a regular game we played, mimicking a real date that was happening around us while we ate. There was no malice in our theatrics, only lighthearted fun. The girl had bleach blond hair pulled back in a messy bun, and the boy was wearing a pale pink V-neck. They were deep in shallow conversation.

Brooke put on her best Valley girl voice. "So, what are you studying? Something manly that will make a lot of money one day, I hope."

"Oh, just bro-science, you know," I said, lowering my voice a few octaves.

"That's super cool . . ."

Several feet away the girl started to giggle, and Brooke continued.

"Ha, ha, ha, you'll have to excuse me, I'm just nervous, and your breath smells like a year-old taco. Did you eat a taco around this time last year?"

I laughed out loud and the game was over.

As the year progressed, the thought of eating cheese on a tortilla became more and more revolting. Around March, I stopped eating foods that were obviously fattening.

Salad dressing: *Could I have mine on the side?*

Cheese: *No, thank you.*

Mayonnaise: *Are you insane?*

From there, the list kept growing. By May I had cut out all dairy products, carbs, sugars, and most meat. Before long my diet consisted entirely of fruits, vegetables, brown rice, and almond milk. Even then, when I was consuming the same nutrients as a ten-pound rabbit, I convinced myself I was being healthy. My self-esteem had become directly connected to the food I ate—

vegetables made me feel strangely empowered, whereas the foods I had blacklisted immediately turned into self-loathing in my mouth. At one point, I replaced up to two meals a day with carrots. My body fought back, turning my palms orange. Other people began noticing my weight loss and commented on how skinny I looked, usually out of concern, but I took it as a compliment. *Thank you for noticing*, I thought. And I thought of little else, spending more and more time staring at my reflection in the mirror—standing sideways, one hand on my stomach and the other on the small of my back.

"I feel so fat." The words finally materialized one evening in July.

Brooke looked at me like I had rats crawling out of my ears.

"What are you talking about? You're so skinny!"

"My stomach isn't as flat as it used to be. I'm so wide from the side, I look like a cow."

"Whatever, you look great," she said, brushing it off. But it was the first of many conversations we would have in front of the mirror, until it became the only conversation we had—me complaining about my appearance, Brooke telling me I was skinny, and neither of us having anything else left to say.

One night, after a long week of studying, Brooke ran into our room waving several pieces of paper back and forth in her hand.

"Lindsey! I got an A on my Biochemistry test! A ninety-one but that's still an A!"

"That's awesome!" I said, smiling for the first time all day.

She was ecstatic.

"I'm taking the night off from studying. Want to go celebrate with me?"

"Yes!"

"Let's go to Guru's!" She said it like she was sharing a gift.

My heart sank. I wanted to go with her, to sit in our corner booth and giggle like children, but she'd want me to share the meal.

My mind raced.

Should I go? I don't have to order anything. I could just keep her company. But what if she offers to share? I'll want to eat some. But the grease, the cheese. No, it's not worth it. I can't go. I need an excuse but it has to be good, believable. But she'll be so disappointed . . .

I looked up and watched Brooke finger through the test, beaming from ear to ear. Every part of me wanted to go, but something stronger was holding me back.

I made an excuse, and she went with Kelsey instead.

Later she brought me home half her quesadilla, and it sat in the fridge until she finally threw it away. I think that's when we stopped sharing things. If I was in our room, she usually wasn't. I stopped wearing her clothes, I couldn't eat any of the food she liked, and I didn't feel like I fit in with our roommates or friends anymore. Brooke even got her own car. Distance slowly spread between all aspects of our relationship, and neither of us knew the cause or how to confront it. So we didn't.

Brooke busied herself most weekends so I often went out alone—not that it mattered. By that point I'd become so consumed with myself that when I went to parties I focused more on the food and body types in the room than I did on the actual people. *Where's the food table? What kind of things should I avoid? Who is the skinniest girl in this room? How do I compare? What kind of dressing is on that salad? How many miles would it take to run off that cookie?* As abnormal as these thoughts may seem, they had come on so gradually that I didn't recognize the invasion. They started as gap fillers— the things I thought about when I wasn't interacting with other people—until these filler thoughts became all I had left.

"I look so fat!" I said for the umpteenth time one morning before class.

Brooke looked down from the top bunk at my reflection in the mirror and scowled.

"Lindsey, what is wrong with you?"

I lifted my shirt to look at my stomach.

"Are you blind?" she asked. "Look at yourself in the mirror. You're skinnier than ninety-nine percent of the human population!"

She was practically yelling now.

I turned sideways, ignoring her reproach.

"Just . . . *STOP!*"

Maybe I ate too much cereal. Half a bowl next time, I thought.

Brooke crawled down from the bed, the wood protesting with each step, and left me standing in front of the mirror alone. I didn't notice.

I'd always lived a colorful life, but in the following months my world became gray, the color of the dirty snow that lined the streets outside my window. One night in early September I returned home from work and sat down on my bed feeling utterly defeated. It had been a terrible day, for no particular reason other than it just felt so. In the next room I heard Brooke laughing. Cassie was probably telling a funny story about her latest date, or maybe Kelsey was practicing a striptease again. It didn't matter. I couldn't think of a good reason to ever get off the bed again. After a few minutes, or maybe even hours—I don't recall—Brooke came into our room quietly, sat down at her desk, and began doing homework. I watched her work silently across the room and felt the pain of my ordinary day tenfold. I longed for her to tell me what was so funny in the other room, to tell me anything. But as I looked at her I realized we were hardly more than strangers. I understand now how insidious denial is. I ached for the relationship I had lost with my sister, my best friend, and yet it never occurred to me that my obsession with food was part of the problem—probably because I didn't even know I had an obsession. The only thing my denial couldn't hide from me was the reality of my loss in the moment. Something was terribly wrong in my life.

Some days I went to social events out of obligation and pretended to have fun; some days I stayed in bed, because I couldn't think of a reason to get up; some days I left class early because my stomach wouldn't stop growling. Most days I came home and felt alone for reasons I couldn't explain, and every day I unknowingly used food as an escape—limiting my food intake, and watching my body respond. My routine included weighing myself twenty times a day and scrutinizing every curve in the mirror, complaining about my appearance, and hating myself. No one would have guessed I cried myself to sleep most nights. I lost weight, I lost confidence, and ultimately, I lost myself.

I must have hit my breaking point when I finally called my mom and explained how I felt.

"I cry for no reason. I don't want to go out, and I'd rather just sleep than do anything else. I don't even know who I've become."

There was a pause. Then she replied, "Lindsey, what you're describing sounds like depression."

My mom had dealt with depression her entire life, and I grew up watching Jennifer struggle with the same disorder. Still, the thought that I too was depressed seemed ludicrous. No, I didn't have depression. That was their battle, not mine. I tried to brush off the notion, but it lingered. Later, the conversation resurfaced.

"Maybe your diet is affecting your mood," my mom said carefully. "I know you like to eat healthy, but you need to do it right, so you get enough nutrition."

She suggested I eat nuts, because they were high in good fats. She told me to eat cheese occasionally, for protein, and she recommended I use olive oil sparingly in my cooking. All I heard was *fats*, *cheese*, and *oil*. The thought of changing my diet made me panic and I kept thinking, *I can't do that, I can't eat that!* The anxiety in my mind startled me, and for the first time I realized I hadn't always thought about food this way. I hadn't always obsessed over it. I hadn't always feared it.

"I think about it all the time," I confided.

"About what?" she asked.

"Food."

There was a pause.

"Lindsey, that's not normal."

"I know," I said. "I think there's something wrong. I think I have a problem."

The line went quiet, and then my mom replied, "Okay, we can work with that. I love you. It's going to be okay."

By that point I was crying, which was nothing new.

"I want to be happy again."

These tears felt heavier on my cheeks, like they'd been building for years.

"You will," she said. "We'll figure it out, okay?"

"Okay."

LIFE
WITH ED

I tried to leave my eating disorder in Utah over Thanksgiving break, but the little bastard jumped in the car and came home with me anyway. Of course, I still thought of it as more of a nuisance than a real problem, so it wasn't a big deal. *Fine, you can come. But keep quiet and don't embarrass me.*

On the night I arrived, my family was sitting around the dinner table when Jennifer made a harmless comment about the abundance of natural sugar in certain fruits. She had recently become enthralled with nutrition and was excited to share her newfound knowledge with anyone who would listen.

"Fruit is good for you," she began, "but did you know even too much fruit can cause a sugar overload in your bloodstream?"

I set down my fork and felt the panic rise in my chest.

"Oh, and get this, sugar turns into fat. So they're finding that it's actually the extra sugar in a person's diet that causes them to gain weight."

"Why are you telling us this? I don't want to hear about the ways fruit can be bad for me."

"I just thought it was interesting."

"Well, it's not."

"Okay, why are you being—"

"Just stop!"

Jennifer looked stunned, and everyone at the table slowly stopped chewing. I remember looking down at my plate, hating everything on it, hating myself.

"I'm sorry," I said quietly.

A tear fell onto my fork, and I left the table before anyone could respond. I was twenty-three years old, and I had just yelled at my sister over strawberries. It was insane. Was I insane?

An hour or so later my mom knocked on my bedroom door.

"Can I come in?"

She sat down next to me on the bed.

"I called Gail Baker and got the name of Kendall's nutritionist," she said.

Kendall was a girl we knew who was anorexic in high school. I understood what my mom was saying.

"I got you an appointment for tomorrow morning. Will you go?"

I was too embarrassed to argue.

The nutritionist's name was Catherine, and her office smelled like clean laundry and peach candles. I sat down and she started by saying, "So are you going to have a big Thanksgiving dinner with your family?"

I smiled. "Yes, we always do."

"So what's your plan?" she asked casually.

"Excuse me?"

"Your plan. What you are going to eat, what you'll avoid, and what you are going to do before and after the meal. You've thought about it already, haven't you?"

I had never considered it a plan—that sounded strange—but now that she brought it up, I did have one. For weeks I had been eating "healthier" than usual and exercising more frequently. Of course I wanted to indulge in a little delicious food—but more than that, I knew I would have to eat in front of my family, specifically my worried mother. I wanted to prepare my body for the onslaught of extra calories. For starters, I was going to get up and run in the morning before the meal. At dinner I would eat mostly lean white turkey, definitely no sweet potato casserole, no sparkling cider, minimal gravy, one roll, and a lot of green beans. I would say I was too full to have pie. Later that afternoon, while everyone was napping, I would go on another jog. As strange as her question was, it made me recognize the reality of my problem, and more important, that I wasn't alone—that I wasn't some kind of freak. There were other people who thought about food the same way I did. There had to be, or she wouldn't have asked the question.

When I went back to school the following week, I promised my mom I would visit the free counseling center, more for her than for me, of course. The university didn't have an eating disorder specialist, but the therapist told me about a new support group for girls with similar problems, so I went.

In the room there was a stage. To the right, a life-size cutout of Elvis winked at us, and in front of the curtain a chest of props sat open, exposing its contents—blond wigs, plastic swords, a purple stuffed leopard. None of us noticed these things at our first meeting. We only saw one another: calves, thighs, hips, stomachs, arms, and cheeks.

Our group leader said she had chosen the theater room for the meetings because it was a place where people could "shed who they are and become who they want to be." It was also in the basement, where no one was likely to interrupt. We felt like well-kept secrets—all of us in baggy shirts on a stage built for amateurs.

At our second meeting only half of us returned. We went around the circle and took turns telling our stories. One of us had an obese mother who couldn't walk farther than the mailbox: *I don't want to become my mom.* One of us hadn't had a period in three years: *I probably won't be able to have kids.* One of us was so skinny, it looked like the weight of her skin was too much for her spine, and one of us was overweight and couldn't look anyone in the eye. One of us was molested as a child and liked having control over her own body: *Food was the one thing I could control, and now it's controlling me.*

When it was my turn, I didn't have any explanation or a traumatic experience. I told my simple story and sobbed until my words were inaudible. I cried for nothing, and for everything. At first I couldn't understand why I was so emotional. What did I have to be upset about? In hindsight, I realize it was the first time I had referred to "my problem" as an eating disorder out loud to anyone other than my mom, and I think part of me was grieving a loss.

For several weeks, going to these meetings was a constant internal struggle. I felt exposed, scrutinized, and damaged. I didn't want to be in a roomful of people with problems, and I certainly didn't want to be considered one of them. I thought I could handle my issues on my own. That's what the demon wants us to believe. He's a big bad guy who preys on our weaknesses and uses our isolation to his advantage. For months I thought about skipping the meetings or doing things on my own, but I also thought about my demon and his desire to take me down. And then I got in my car and drove to the dramatic arts building where I talked, listened, and gave the big bad guy my big bad middle finger. In the long run, group therapy turned out to be the most helpful of all the treatments I went through. All the dirty props aside, I loved the theater room. It was the one place I felt understood. It was the one place I didn't have to lie to other people or to myself.

Some days we talked about our pasts, some days we talked about our goals, some days we talked about boys, friends, and our mothers. Jaime's mom told her if she didn't go to a therapist she would cut off her tuition payments. Sarah's mom sent her self-help books on eating disorders without ever bringing it up. Rachel's mom started giving her $300 a month to buy healthy food. My mom called me a few times a week to check in. I knew she wanted to ask about my progress—it lingered in the back of her throat. Instead, she asked me about school, work, and my music. Even still, I understood her floating questions and unspoken pleas.

"How are you today?" *Are you eating well?*

"How are your classes?" *Are you still going to your group?*

"Just wanted to say I love you." *Please don't give up.*

Eventually I tried private therapy but I didn't connect with any of my counselors. They were always searching for the same thing: a reason. I didn't have one, and my lack of an explanation made me feel like a misfit in dealing with my own problems. Although I continued to go to my private sessions, my mom became the best counselor I had. She didn't search for a reason. She just listened, and over time I taught her how to respond.

Don't tell me I look good, I know that means I've gained weight.

Don't ask me if I'm eating well, it stresses me out.

At first she said all the wrong things and I reacted in all the wrong ways. But I learned to trust her more than I trusted myself.

One of the best books I've ever read about eating disorders is called *Life Without Ed.* In a nutshell, it is the story of a girl who, at the request of her therapist, names her eating disorder Ed. This concept changed everything I had previously thought about myself. For the first time I was able to separate my eating disorder from my personality. I realized that all the negative thoughts I had about myself were not my own, they were coming from Ed, and my eating disorder was an unhealthy relationship I could get rid of. I too had conversations in my head with my eating disorder. It told me lies, and I called them out.

At first, I felt like I had a split personality. Every time I ate something out of my comfort zone the internal battle would begin in my head. Automatically, the eating disorder side of my brain would say, *You can't even say "no" to a small bowl of ice cream? You are pathetic and weak.* To combat these thoughts I searched for the logical side of my brain, which would say, *Good job, Lindsey. You are fighting against the eating disorder. You are strong.*

For the next few years, every snack, meal, or thought about food instigated an argument in my head—sometimes one I didn't feel strong enough to have. But I knew that not fighting meant losing, so I challenged my disorder. I reasoned with it, and over time I retrained my brain how to think. My eating disorder no longer controls me, but every once in a while it tries to come back into my mind. It says:

You will be happier if you don't go out to eat with your friends.

A cookie will undo an entire week's worth of exercise.

I can see the extra chocolate on your hips.

I say, "You're lying."

As part of my treatment I was only allowed to weigh myself once a week. By this time I had accepted the fact that I needed to gain weight, but every time I saw the needle go up I felt sick inside. Even when I stayed off the scale I noticed every extra pound. My sunken cheeks started to fill in, the natural curve of my stomach returned, and there was a new softness to the skin protecting my ribs and hips. One pound, two pounds, five pounds. I felt each one invade my body and I resisted the urge to fight back. I fought for myself, for my family, and because I knew I was a better person when I did. Our demon wants us to believe we are too weak, too sad, or too far-gone; but he's also a big fat liar so you shouldn't believe a word he says. Throughout my entire life I had been taught—and on my mission *I* taught—about God's love. But it wasn't until this time that I realized how disconnected I had become. I wanted my life back more than anything, but I wasn't strong enough to make the changes on my own. I had to rediscover myself in God's eyes: I was a daughter of God, He created me, and He thought I was beautiful.

From then on, at every meal, I prayed over my food, *Thank you for this meal I am so blessed to have*; and every morning I looked my reflection in the eye, *Thank you for this body, I am beautiful*. I wasn't very sincere at first, but I think He understood.

When I broke one hundred pounds again I was twenty-four years old. I mentally congratulated myself, as I watched a tear hit the scale.

While I was first grappling with my disorder, I did a lot of research to better understand what was happening in my mind and my body. In the process, I read that anorexia was an incurable disease. *Incurable*. What a horrible little word. I want to squash that word beneath my Birkenstock knockoffs. I was not born with anorexia, and it is not a physical condition made up of cells. On the contrary, it is a developed way of thinking, made up inside the mind. My mind is not some predetermined scientific space, where change is impossible and anorexia is incurable. Yes, now and then thoughts related to my eating disorder resurface—usually in response to added stress or changes in my life—but I've learned to distinguish these unhealthy thoughts from the healthy ones before they have a chance to affect my life. I can control them before they control me. If anorexia was really incurable, I'd still weigh ninety-two pounds—isolated in a world controlled by food and distorted versions of myself. I'm not that person anymore. I don't live in that world anymore. I hate the thought that someone, somewhere might read about their "incurable eating disorder" and believe it to be the truth. That's why I'm telling you, it's not. So hang in there, it's worth it. *You're* worth it.

AMERICA'S GOT IT,
I WANT IT

I never imagined I would be the kind of person to collapse in tears onto a public restroom floor. Especially not at twenty-three years old. I guess you can't really know how you'll handle heartbreak until it's upon you.

My experience with *America's Got Talent* was dreadful. I know, surprise, surprise. Besides the fact that I got berated on national television, being part of *America's Got Talent* was emotionally draining in a way that made me question my sanity. I can't be too cynical, considering it was Piers Morgan's insult and Sharon Osbourne's doubt that motivated me to keep trying. That is, after I scraped myself off the bathroom floor. I'm getting ahead of myself. Let's back up.

I was a junior in college when I heard about *America's Got Talent* tryouts and, of course, I called my mom. When I asked her if I should audition she didn't even pause.

"Absolutely! Can I come with you?"

I think I knew she'd say that, which is why I called her first. I bought a plane ticket, and my mom met me in Los Angeles. For several hours we waited in a long line of America's finest. I was sick with nerves, but watching a Michael Jackson impersonator practice spinning on his roller skates all day did wonders for my mood.

Waiting for a response was agony, but a few tedious months later I was invited back to LA for the first round of taping. I couldn't call my mom fast enough. I was going to be on national television!

In preparation for my next audition, I was determined to overcome the added stress of playing in front of a crowd. Since I didn't have any big crowds at my disposal, I did something even more stressful: I went door to door in my apartment complex and did private performances for complete strangers.

With my iPod speakers in one hand and my violin in the other, I explained that I had a big audition and needed to practice my stage presence. Surprisingly enough, everyone I approached invited me inside. Seconds later, I was attempting backbends and twirls in their living rooms to a barely audible backtrack. Most of them avoided eye contact, and if they were cute boys, I did, too. I figured if I could handle something that uncomfortable, I could take any reaction that came at me onstage.

When I got back to LA for rehearsals, I fell quickly into the trap we call reality TV. I won't go into too much detail, but I will say the experience in general felt more like a prison than a television show. In the space below please insert your own assumptions about how reality TV is handled behind the scenes.

_____

_____

_____

My guess is you're probably pretty close to the truth. I wish I could say I was above it all, but my self-esteem hung in the balance every day. *America's Got Talent* became the only thing that mattered, and if I couldn't succeed there—if they didn't want me—who would?

After going through several auditions, I made it to the quarterfi-
nals. It was really happening! I had three months to prepare for my
next performance, and I practiced like my life depended on it, over
and over and over again. I was still learning how to dance while I
played so I practiced the ears off my roommates and twirled my way
through every apartment in Provo.

Before I knew it the week of prep before the live show had
arrived. At this point I also got to know the other contestants as
more than my competition. Murray Sawchuck was one of the best
magicians I have ever seen. More than that, he was the voice of
reason when I was surrounded by uncertainty. He was a veteran in
show business, and he reminded me often that *America's Got Talent*
was nothing but a giant game—if I lost, I could always play somewhere else.

"Just be dramatic. Act like it's your one chance and say what they
want to hear. It's a game, but two can play."

I didn't want to play games—I wanted to play my violin. I
wanted to win based on talent. Besides, I really did believe it was my
one and only chance.

A few nights later, I got onstage and performed for America. We
all know what happened next, and if you don't you can watch it on
the Internet. But to this day I can't listen to that Kesha song without
hearing the sound of a buzzer in the middle of the chorus. It took
everything I had not to cry onstage as, one by one, the judges broke
me down on national television. Sharon Osbourne said what I was
doing wouldn't be enough to fill a theater in Vegas, and Piers Morgan told me I sounded like "a bunch of rats being strangled." It was
the first time anyone had ever been mean to me for the sake of being
mean. I think this says a lot about how I grew up, and it's a gift I
wish bestowed on every human being in this world. I guess if that
was the worst treatment I had encountered so far in my life, things
were going pretty well. But heartache is relative, and worse than the

humiliation was the fact that I thought my dreams were coming to an end.

When the lights faded I held it together until I reached the bathroom, where I locked the door, sank to the floor, and sobbed. I was humiliated, but more than anything, I felt utterly betrayed by God. Leading up to my performance, I was confident it was nothing short of divine intervention that had led me there—that God wanted me to do well. Instead of rising to the top as I had prayed for, I took a nosedive, and I couldn't understand why.

At the end of the night I walked slowly outside to meet my family, each step heavier than the last. I knew what they would say—about my performance being great despite what the judges had said—and I rehearsed simple responses in my head. *Thanks, mom* or *That's very sweet.*

They were huddled at the street corner to my right: my mom on the phone, Brooke talking to Marina, and my cousin and Jennifer holding posters with my name in red glitter. I was so focused on not crying, I almost didn't notice my dad ahead of the group, walking in my direction. He reached me quickly, wrapped his arms around my shoulders, and whispered, "I am *so* proud of you."

I hadn't prepared a response for that, so I didn't say anything. I just let his words sink in, like the tears I left on his sleeve.

On the way out of the parking lot my dad's car broke down, so we walked to a nearby IHOP and waited for a tow truck. I remember sitting in the corner booth, trying to hold it together in front of my family and our middle-aged waitress. In an effort to distract myself I told my eating disorder to shove it, and I ordered a tall chocolate milkshake. When I finished the last sip, my defiance dissolved into self-loathing and I cried even harder. *Why did I eat that? Why did I come here? I'm so fat, so ugly.* My demons were at the top of their game. Jennifer, however, went to every table in the restaurant asking everyone to vote for me. Based on my performance, I already knew it was over. But as you know by now, Jennifer never quits before the finish line.

The next night I got back up onstage and faced the judges, the audience, and America as they called someone else's name. I had come so close, and for months I had been carrying this secret fantasy around, imagining all the ways my life would change for the better. I didn't have a Plan B. This was my one chance, and it was gone as quickly as it had come.

Hours earlier, I was the center of focus, and I could practically feel the spotlight waiting to fall on me. The problem was, all this attention fell into my lap at once, and I was like a balloon filled with air. When the balloon suddenly popped, I was left more torn, empty, and shriveled than when I started.

People often tell me how smart I was for not signing a contract with a record label, but the truth is, I was never given the option. I didn't have anything to sign or not sign, because no one wanted me. I think God was trying to say, "Just hold on a minute, I have so much more in store if you'll be patient." I wasn't patient at first, but I didn't give up. And, eventually, my plans did line up with His. *America's Got Talent* was only the first step, a learning experience. Had I won the show, I would have signed *anything* out of desperation. I thank God daily that it was never a choice, because I would have made the wrong one. After being eliminated, I had to start over from scratch, which turned out to be one of the biggest blessings in my music career. Working from the ground up gave me the time I needed to learn the value of my identity as a musician and a human. Moving forward, I realized I didn't want anyone to tell me how to dress, what song to play, or how to do my hair and makeup ever again. I didn't want to be a puppet, and I decided I would never submit to someone else's opinion above my own. If I was going to continue in the music world, I would do it on my terms.

When the media and my fans praise me for creating such a strong platform on my own, I have to remind myself that it was never my idea. The big man upstairs had my back the whole time. After *America's Got Talent*, I imagine He was up there saying, "Slow down," or "This is not the end," or "Will someone get this girl an apple!"

No matter what He said, He was up there.

On the day following my elimination I was waiting by Gate 32B in the Los Angeles International Airport to fly back to Utah. A man leaned over my shoulder from behind and whispered, with a thick Mexican accent, "I voted for you." I smiled and said, "Thank you," as he slowly backed away. It was simultaneously the sweetest and the creepiest thing anyone has ever said to me.

WHAT HAPPENS
IN VEGAS

Following my experience on *America's Got Talent*, I took a short hiatus from my violin. My confidence was on the mend, but the thought of stepping onto another stage still left me feeling panicked and embarrassed. I wallowed in self-pity for a healthy amount of time, and then I got back to work. In the fall of 2010 I took my first big step back into the music scene by auditioning at a collegiate showcase. It was an opportunity to be seen by a variety of college event planners from all over the country, and I took comfort in knowing that none of them were going to interrupt my performance with an earsplitting buzzer, or critique me in front of a national audience. They were either going to hire me, or they weren't.

In the following months several universities booked me for different events, and I got the added experience of performing on college campuses all over the country. I never knew exactly what I was heading into, but more often than not, I was scheduled to perform in the cafeteria. I've played in a lot of unique settings, but there's nothing quite like getting the lunchtime slot in a food court. I didn't understand why I had been brought hundreds of miles to play for distracted students, but the more events I played, the less I cared. Prior to a performance at the University of Connecticut, the announcer introduced me with a myriad of false information. Among other things, she stated that I was the *winner* of *America's Got Talent*. I remember forcing a smile and thinking, *If that were true I don't think I would be playing next to the Taco Bell counter at noon on a Wednesday*. When she finished, I gritted my teeth and stepped out on the two-foot riser in front of thirty people, half of whom were standing in various fast-food lines, while the other half were absorbed in lunchtime banter. At first, this kind of audience was discouraging, but I took it as a challenge. I played louder and danced harder to fight for their attention. *Hey! Can your tuna sandwich do this?* At the end of every set, I bowed and told the remaining bystanders they could find a few of my covers on YouTube.

The compensation I received for my college performances was decent, but I had to pay for my own travel and accommodations most of the time. To maximize profit, I frequently slept in my rental car or at the airport. In case you have never had the opportunity to spend the night in an airport, I'll let you in on a little secret: that's when all the monster vacuums come out. At first it was a nuisance, but after three back-to-back shows in different states, I became so tired that not even the cleaning staff could keep me awake.

When I wasn't traveling to random college events I was still taking a full load of courses at BYU and working part-time. I used the money from my day job to get by, and I put every penny I earned from performing back into my music. I installed a pickup on my violin, got a sound pedal so I could control my settings onstage, bought a new bow, and that November I started working with a producer named Marco G. on original music. We spent hours together developing backtracks, and then I wrote and recorded the melody. When we were done I had spent two thousand dollars on three tracks: "Spontaneous Me," "Song of the Caged Bird," and "Transcendence." Besides my tuition, it was the most money I'd ever spent on anything, and self-doubt was my steady companion. It reminded me of all the other places my money could have gone, as well as the unlikelihood that anyone would buy my music. In spite of these insecurities, I continued to save my money and write music. In April 2011, I returned to the studio to put together a few more tracks.

Eventually, I set up a website and started getting offers from other event planners. That's when I found out how difficult it was to determine my own value. I always hated discussing payment with prospective clients, so I frequently pretended to be my own manager, "Jerry." Jerry answered all my e-mails about money, but even *he* wasn't comfortable asking for enough pay or negotiating contracts. As a result, Jerry and I were frequently overworked and undercompensated. The first gig Jerry booked for me paid two hundred dollars plus accommodations to fly out of state for a corporate business event. Jerry also agreed to have me travel several hours to play at a child's birthday party. This went on for months until I got an offer to play at the MGM Grand in Las Vegas. Finally, a gig I could say out loud without turning red in the face. To save money I planned on driving from Provo to Vegas, but the day before the show, my car started rattling.

The following morning I barely made it to the bus station on time, and when I boarded the Greyhound almost all the seats were taken. Finally, I spotted a seat in the very back, covered in bags. The woman who owned the luggage glared at me as I approached, but she and I both knew my options were few.

"I'm sorry, but I really need to be on this bus. Can I sit here?" I asked cautiously. After a few uncomfortable seconds, she moved her things to the floor, and I was safely on my way to Sin City.

At the first rest stop I got off the bus to stretch my legs, mentally agonizing over the remaining four hours of my trip. *Why am I doing this? Are these gigs worth all the time and effort it takes to get to them? And for what? A few distracted listeners in a cafeteria or a club?* Suddenly, the direction of my life seemed pointless. I succumbed once again to exhaustion and despair. This dream was impractical, and this lifestyle lonely. I needed to just finish college, get a real job, and move on. As I sat back down in my seat, I noticed the woman next to me hadn't moved, but the scowl was gone from her face. *She must be getting close to her stop*, I thought. When I nonchalantly asked her where she was headed she told me she was traveling to California to visit a daughter she hadn't seen in seven years. Her name was Debra, and to my surprise, she had already been on different buses for three days. She was recently divorced, had just been laid off, and was facing a future of uncertainty and a past of regret. "So," she said slowly, "I'm picking up what I got left and moving forward, doing some things I should have done a long time ago." As she spoke I couldn't help but wonder. If I gave up on my dream, would I find myself on a Greyhound in seven years, talking to a stranger about *doing some things I should have done a long time ago*? When we parted ways, I thanked her for letting me have the seat, and I wished her the best for the remainder of her ride.

That night I played at the MGM's Studio 54 with DJ Loczi. Loczi was nice enough, but I knew immediately this was not a scene I wanted to frequent. As the night continued, barely dressed dancers joined me onstage, and the number of wasted men in the audience multiplied. They pointed, they drooled, and they shouted things not worth repeating. I could have been playing the kazoo in a cow suit and they wouldn't have noticed, so long as my dancer friends were on the stage to provide the real entertainment. I wanted to grab the girls by the shoulders and yell, "You're better than this! Go find your clothes and your self-respect!" Instead, they did booty shakes and danced on poles. At the end of the night I was all too happy to close my set and go back to my room. The gig sounded more legit than most from a business point of view, and the money was better, but I knew I wouldn't be returning. College cafeterias, here I come.

In the morning, the event coordinator stopped by my room to thank me for playing and cordially asked me what time my flight was leaving. When I told her I was taking the bus, she looked at me in horror.

"You rode a Greyhound? How did you stomach that?"

Riding the Greyhound wasn't my first choice, either, but her aversion to it upset me. I felt defensive—for Debra, and for the other people on the same bus with their own reasons for being there. She offered to have her assistant book me a flight home on their tab, but I refused on principle. I thought of my dad traveling the country in a disheveled camper and the people he met—people like Debra who had stories to share—and I politely declined her offer. I *wanted* to take the bus. I probably won't have a reason to ride a Greyhound anytime soon, but I'm glad I did then. Had I not gotten a reality check from Debra, I might have given up. Wherever you are, Debra, I hope you found that place you were moving toward. With your help, I found mine.

BLAME IT
ON THE BOYS

Sometimes I worry about becoming a cat lady, and I don't even like cats. Aside from their superior attitudes, feline hygiene in general disgusts me. Covering yourself in saliva is not an acceptable substitute for a bath. Obviously, I prefer men to cats, but my lifestyle makes it difficult for me to meet that single, hunky, funny, talented, intellectual, supportive, family-oriented, stylish, religious guy I'm looking for. Even before I started touring, I had trouble finding a man I could see myself sharing toothpaste with on a daily basis. But it's not for lack of trying.

During my final semester of college I developed a magnetic aura that attracted everyone within one hundred miles who had a single cousin, brother, roommate, neighbor, or uncle. From every side people closed in on me, trying to play matchmaker and rescue me from a future of cleaning litter boxes in old age. I still don't know what possessed me to agree to all those blind dates. It probably had something to do with my hopeless romantic belief that saying no could mean missing out on my soul mate. Most of these setups were perfectly normal boys with whom I simply had nothing in common, but occasionally they turned out to be genuine doughheads. People always thought they knew someone perfect for me—which frequently turned out to be offensive once I got to know my dates. I'm going to share a few stories with you now in hopes that it will save some other single girl from a similar experience. Gentlemen, this chapter is a "what not to do" guide of sorts, so listen up.

One of the more memorable evenings started at a grocery store, where my date surprised me by saying, "Tonight, we are going to buy ingredients to make dinner."

"Sounds good," I replied, remaining optimistic.

"But there is one catch," he said, pausing dramatically. "We can only use *this*!" He pulled out four dirty quarters and jingled them in front of my face.

"Okay . . ." I said with a forced smile.

"But don't worry," he went on, "we can go back to your apartment and use anything there to make dinner as well."

In case you're as confused as I was at this point, I'll break it down for you. This boy took me to a grocery store, gave me his extra laundry change to buy "dinner," and then invited himself back to *my* apartment to eat *my* food. What a Romeo.

Since this was probably the worst date I had ever been on, the last thing I wanted to do was take him back to meet my roommates, but I couldn't see a way around it. We ended up buying instant pudding with his stupid dollar and went back to my apartment to find real food. When we walked in the door, Mackenzie and Kelsey were doing homework at the kitchen table. At the sight of my date they both assumed our evening was going well. While he rummaged through my pantry, they gestured thumbs-up and mouthed things like, "He's cute!" and "Way to go!" I appreciated their enthusiasm, but while his back was turned I made a few gestures of my own.

Then there was the guy whose idea of a creative date was making me sit in a wheelchair the *entire* night. It started out innocently enough. He picked me up, opened my door, and drove me to a restaurant. The conversation was fine, and I thought I was in for a relaxing evening. However, as I was about to get out of the car, he held up a hand and said, "Before you get out I have a small surprise." He ran around to the trunk and met me at my door, with a wheelchair.

"You get to spend the evening in a wheelchair," he said beaming, as if he were whisking me off to Paris. If someone were to pull this on me today I would simply say, "No thanks," but I had never been faced with such a ridiculous request. Before I knew what was happening, I was sitting in a wheelchair! It was horrifying, sitting there, knowing full well I was masquerading as disabled. And did I mention he took me to a buffet? This presented a whole host of additional problems. I spent far too much time trying to maneuver in and out of buffet lines and tables, not to mention that I couldn't see any of the food choices.

"Are there nuts in that salad?" I asked, craning my neck to see what was in each tray. "I'll just have that."

As you can imagine, I didn't dare attempt to go back for seconds. I did, however, need to use the bathroom. I awkwardly wheeled myself over to the restrooms where I sat in front of the closed door for a full minute before deciding to stand up and leave the chair in the hall. Following this humiliating experience, he took me to a bowling alley. Back in the chair, I spent the rest of the evening aiming a ball down a metal track they brought out to accommodate me. It was embarrassing enough having special treatment when I knew I didn't need it, but the thought of anyone noticing that I was faking was even more daunting. As I sat there, trying not to move too much, I wondered, *Is the "problem" in my back or my legs? Wait, what? This is so wrong!*

Admittedly, I did my share of *being* the bad date in college. One time, Marina and I hitched a ride to Utah with a friend of a friend. He was incredibly attractive, and the first half hour of the drive was full of witty conversation. *This could really turn into something*, I thought. Unfortunately, I spent the last ten and a half hours periodically asking him to pull over so I could puke on the side of the road.

Thankfully, I was able to fall asleep, only to wake myself up with a fart minutes later. There is no recovering from that.

At the next pit stop, Marina and I were in the bathroom when she lamented my sickness. "Girl, I'm so sorry you're sick," she said in her thick Russian accent. "But that was really embarrassing. Like, really embarrassing. I was dying in the backseat. Like really, really, really—"

"I get it! I'm a farting, barfing embarrassment."

Marina has never been much for sugarcoating. We got back in the car, where I continued to embarrass her for the remainder of the drive. Several weeks after our trip, we tried to invite the guy over for dinner in an effort to salvage what was left of my reputation. He was busy—most likely with a girl who hadn't made a Dutch oven out of the confined space of his car. If you're reading this now, attractive friend of a friend, my dinner offer still stands.

While these dates were definite busts, I'll give my eating disorder credit for ruining any real chance for love in general. Even if the guys were nice and interesting I wouldn't have noticed, so long as the night involved eating dinner, dessert, or—worst-case scenario—both. I had a hard enough time finding food I felt comfortable eating at the grocery store. The chances of finding something that met my standards at a restaurant were slim to none. While they talked about their jobs or hobbies, I panicked about the fat in my meal and the best way to eat around it. I can't tell you how many times I was escorted into the Pizza Pie Cafe feeling like a prisoner, the panic in my chest rising as my date piled slice after greasy slice on his plate, expecting me to do the same.

One time, my date looked at my small helping and said, "Is that all you're going to have? It's all-you-can-eat, don't be shy."

I'm not shy, you moron. I'm anorexic.

In spite of these distractions I did manage to date a few normal dudes in college. John Doe was my official boyfriend for only four months. In that time, everyone I knew fell in love with him—except for me. In fact, when I broke it off I think Brooke was more upset than I was. He was charming, muscular, and had a smile that would melt your face off. Aside from the obvious physical attraction, John was also one of the most genuinely kind people I have ever met. No matter where we went he made people feel special. As a result, we were upgraded, promoted, and doted on. He was the poor man's millionaire. We didn't get extra perks because we were rich or well known; we got them because he was smoother than a greased cookie sheet. On the flip side, the man was also about as *deep* as a greased cookie sheet. In the middle of a hard day's work, I frequently went over to his place to find him basking in the sun. He'd ask about my day, and I'd tell him about school, work, and my latest music project. When it was his turn, he'd say, "I went to the gym this morning, made a protein shake, practiced some guitar, and now I'm workin' on a little tan." I think that was the part where I was supposed to swoon over his hot bod. Instead, I was thoroughly distracted by trying to figure out how he could possibly spend an entire day working out and tanning. I knew it was officially over when he told me his mom had never missed a day at the gym.

There was another guy I really liked, and we went out on and off for several months. He was the smart, driven type, and he had a face like Edward Cullen—cold and sparkly. When he finally kissed me, I came home and told my roommates. They screamed the way girlfriends should and demanded details.

"How was it?!"

"Was it like kissing a vampire?"

"Tell us!"

I paused and said, "It was . . . a mom kiss."

He had literally leaned in and touched his lips to mine. I think his tube of ChapStick got more action than I did that night. They say you can tell a lot from your first kiss with someone, and "they" must be right, because that was the end of our relationship. I also dated a cute nerd, Vick, who didn't realize he was a nerd. In fact, he'll probably read this and have no idea I'm talking about him. We had been friends for a very long time. So long, that I had already met his entire family. After I broke up with John and then Mom Kiss, he forcefully told me he was going to be my boyfriend. For a while I thought our relationship was really going somewhere, until he confided that he didn't think he could ever love one person completely. I knew it wasn't true, but I took it as an indication that he probably wouldn't ever love *me* completely. Way to kill the mood, Vick.

I think the thing that upsets me most about my uneventful dating life is the fact that I know I would be an amazing grandmother. I practically am one already! I say things like "You're darn tootin'" and "Don't get caught in your skivvies." I like comfortable shoes, I get cold easily, and I don't eat cookie dough for fear of salmonella poisoning. Now if I could just find a man to make some grandkids, I would be set. I think I'd be a pretty okay mom, too. I love holidays, and if I had my own family, I could stop harassing my tour crew with little parties that none of them really want to attend. At Halloween, my future kids and I will make a haunted house in the garage; at Christmas, we'll dress up as elves and dance for the neighbors; for Valentine's Day, we'll make homemade cards; and on Groundhog Day, we'll take turns digging holes in the backyard and declaring spring. I want to live my life in chaos, surrounded by Mini-Mes who think I'm a weirdo but love me unconditionally. In the meantime, I could settle for a kitten. Just one—or twelve.

YOU HAVE TO
IF YOU WANT TO

When I met Cassie for the first time I was elbow deep in a pot of refried beans. Beans have always been one of my comfort foods, so after I finished unpacking my new college apartment, I called my mom and asked her to walk me through the recipe. After boiling the beans for several hours, the next step is to squish them using a potato masher. The only problem was I didn't own a potato masher. In a pinch, I reached my hands into the pot and began squeezing the beans between my fingers. It was very therapeutic, actually. Seconds later, Cassie walked in the door, and I was mortified. I smiled sheepishly and thought, *Hi, I'm your new roommate. I'd shake your hand, but right now mine are covered in a magical fruit.* She came closer to confirm that I was actually doing what she thought I was doing. Then she said, "Alrighty then," and continued down the hall to her room. I couldn't believe it! I had been there less than twenty-four hours, and I was already the crazy roommate.

A few days later I was sitting at the table eating . . . you guessed it, beans. Cassie entered the kitchen and asked casually, "Hey Lindsey, how are those beans? Remember when I came home and you were squeezing them with your bare hands?"

I dropped my head in shame. "Unfortunately, yes," I said.

She threw her head back and let out one of the greatest laughs I had ever heard. Cassie doesn't giggle or chuckle, she literally HA HAs. Each "HA" is clear and contagious.

In between her laughter, she continued. "I know you're a little weird, because who isn't? But at first I thought you were going to be legit weird—like collect-fingernail-trimmings or sleep-in-the-bathtub weird."

"I didn't have a masher," I whimpered with my head in my hands.

This made her HA HA even louder, and I knew we were going to get along just fine. Later I found out she couldn't sleep without a baby noisemaker, ever. Suddenly, my refried bean incident didn't seem so strange. All my roommates in Apartment 123 were a little weird in their own rights, but our quirks brought us together more than they ever pulled us apart.

Growing up I was always very independent and proud of my individuality. Unfortunately, my eating disorder took that from me. I lost all confidence and didn't know myself well enough to form close relationships. Living in an apartment with so many unique and strong-willed girls helped me to rediscover my personality.

When I started experimenting with hip-hop violin music, I spent hours every day practicing and dancing in front of the mirror in Cassie and Becca's room. (With their permission of course.) Brooke was always studying in our room, and even if she wasn't, the clothes we had strewn all over the floor prevented me from adequately using my dance skills. My dancing was awkward, and my playing was sloppy. Normally, this would have made me feel self-conscious. However, knowing that Kelsey was in the next room practicing the choreography from Beyoncé's music videos in a leotard made me feel completely normal. They accepted everything about me whole-heartedly, and they became my family away from home.

In spite of our close friendship, I can count the number of times I have cried in front of my roommates on three fingers. One night, after a rough day at work I came home in tears. I thought if I kept my head down as I walked through the door no one would notice. Mackenzie was dishing up some of her notorious fart-smelling cheese tortellini in the kitchen. At the sound of the door she turned and lifted her bowl of pasta in the air.

In her best Italian accent she said, "Lindsey! Can I interest you in some-a tortellini de farte?"

I let out a pathetic attempt at a pity laugh, and the smile fell from her face.

"Lindsey? What's wrong?"

I tried to smile, but my lips faltered and a small sob escaped my mouth.

"Oh Mackenzie," I said, "I don't know what's wrong with me."

It was a lie; I knew exactly what was wrong, I just didn't know how to fix it. We talked about the surface issues—the bad day I'd had at work and my frustrations with school. When I was done, she set both hands on the table. "I know exactly what you need."

"What?"

She looked me square in the eyes and said, "Mona." The corners of her mouth turned up into a grin so wide I could have crawled in-side. In a matter of minutes she forced all five of us out of the apart-ment and into her forest-green Toyota Camry.

"Where are we going again?" Brooke asked.

"Mona," Mackenzie replied.

"And what exactly is in Mona?"

"A surprise."

When Mackenzie finally stopped the car thirty minutes later, we were parked in front of a dark clump of trees.

"Follow me," she said, grabbing a flashlight and leading us down a small trail into the dark. When the trees cleared we stopped at the edge of a large, dark pond.

"Welcome to Mona Pond," she said proudly.

"It's lovely," Kelsey spoke in monotone, "but why are we here?"

"To go skinny-dipping, of course," Mackenzie replied. "Don't look!" she yelped as she threw off her clothes and scampered into the black water.

"Mackenzie! You're naked . . . in a pond!" I screamed.

She was swimming from side to side in the dark.

"I know! Trust me, you'll love it."

"Why not?" Cassie said, tossing off her clothes and tiptoeing into the water.

Becca was next, followed by Kelsey, and finally I slipped awkwardly into the pond. After a few minutes, Kelsey got comfortable enough to take a ride on an old rope swing hanging from a lakeside tree. I laughed until I thought I might drown a delightful, naked death.

"Don't you feel better, Linds?" Mackenzie asked.

"Strangely, yes," I replied.

Brooke had stitches on her foot at the time, so she showed her support by stripping down on shore and running circles around six piles of clothes. Cassie's HA HAs skipped across the water and up toward the moon.

From the outside looking in we appeared to be an outgoing and happy group of girls. And we were happy for the most part, but even I didn't realize until much later that each of my roommates were fighting their own battles. One of us was going through heartbreak, one of us had parents who were divorcing, and a couple of us struggled with depression. We didn't openly talk about these things often, but every time one of these burdens got too heavy to bear we returned to Mona. Sometimes we didn't know the exact reason for our visit, but we didn't need to. The only thing that mattered was that one of us needed to get away. No one should have to get away alone, or fully clothed.

Maybe skinny-dipping isn't the most traditional way to deal with problems, but we were never too concerned with social rules. In fact, we eventually made a rulebook for the sole purpose of "throwing it out the window." We kept it on the coffee table, and anytime one of us wanted to do something socially questionable, we wrote it down in the rulebook and did it anyway. Here are some rules to throw out the window in college (or anytime, for that matter) brought to you by the girls of Apartment 123.

Rule #1:   Skinny-dipping is naughty. (MONA BABY!)

Rule #2:   The man has to make the first move. Don't text him unless he texts you. (*Bleh.*)

Rule #3:   You can't wear black with brown. (Says who?)

Rule #4:   Only eat breakfast for breakfast. (As if.)

Rule #5:   Paying for things with all change is tacky. (And functional!)

Rule #6:   Shower every day. (Three days.)

Rule #7:   Don't EVER kiss on a first date. (But if you do, kiss him good.)

Rule #8:   Always get eight hours of sleep. (*Psh!*)

Rule #9:   Don't wear socks with flip-flops. (Umm . . . okay.)

Rule #10: Finish your homework before you play. (Unless something really fun is happening.)

Rule #11: Always wear a bra. (No.)

Rule #12: Glitter is for twelve-year-olds. (And my toenails.)

Rule #13: Don't eat more than your date. (Unless your date is a pansy.)

Rule #14:   When you finish up the last of the powdered milk, you have to mix up another batch. (You don't have to, but it's polite.)

Rule #15:   Eat your veggies. (If you're Lindsey, then stop.)

Rule #16:   If you tell someone your wish it won't come true. (Don't wish on boys, because that won't come true either.)

Rule #17:   No short skirts after forty. (Or before.)

Rule #18:   Never date a man who wears or has worn a jockstrap. (Trust us on this one.)

Rule #19:   Shave your legs once a week in the winter, once a day in the summer. (Or not at all.)

And one last rule that we never threw out the window:

Rule #20:   Always stay in touch with your college roommates. Good friends are hard to come by. (And that's the truth!)

Denny's across from our apartment, at 1:00 A.M. on a Wednesday.

CHAPTER ON MY YOUNG AND CAREFREE DRUG/ALCOHOL ESCAPADES

I have never done drugs or consumed alcohol, so this chapter is really short.

DEVIN
SUPERTRAMP

Brooke and I tried making cookies from scratch once in college. I had a crush on a boy across the hall, and I planned on seducing him with my baking skills. Unfortunately, we added double the baking soda and none of the salt. Since seduction by baked goods was now out of the question, we offered the cookies to Mackenzie instead. She took a big bite and covered her mouth in disgust.

"These are terrible," she said. "I knew it was too good to be true. People don't just give people cookies."

She brought up a good point, and it's a philosophy that has stuck with me. Not long after, a cinematographer named Devin Graham contacted me through YouTube. He wanted to film a music video for me, for free. Naturally I was skeptical. *Okay, what do you want from me, pal?*

He had come across my *America's Got Talent* audition on YouTube, and he e-mailed me about doing a collaboration. As he put it, "I like showcasing interesting talents." He sent me the links to a few of his YouTube videos, and I was blown away. His work was incredible. We continued to correspond, but it all sounded too good to be true—a free video and effortless exposure? What was the catch? He insisted that all he wanted was the rights to put the finished product on his YouTube channel. Devin's equipment was obviously superior to my dad's old camcorder on a tripod, so I accepted.

Once I had a better understanding of how YouTube worked, I realized Devin wasn't just handing out free cookies. As a cinematographer, he needed new material in order to propel his channel. As a hungry musician, I needed opportunities to share my music. We were *exchanging* cookies. I was definitely getting the better end of the bargain so I didn't complain. He told me I could perform whatever I wanted, so I finished up an original recording. A few weeks later, he came to Utah and we spent two days filming my first real YouTube video, "Spontaneous Me."

When Devin picked me up for our first day of filming he arrived in a run-down Subaru. I think it was the first thing that attracted me to him—a successful man in a crappy car, how refreshing (I'm being totally serious). But I liked him for more than his outdated set of wheels. He was the most motivated person I had ever met, and after several hours of filming together, I was sure he was also one of the nicest. Dancing and playing in front of a stranger with a camera that would record my every mistake was intimidating, but Devin had a way of making everything seem easy.

"Just do whatever you would do if I weren't here."

Ignoring the cute guy with the camera in my face was easier said than done, but I trusted him. When we finished filming he invited me to a workshop he was teaching about YouTube.

"I think you would do really well as a YouTuber," he said.

This sounded pretty strange to me. How do you do *well* on YouTube? I already had a few cover videos online with about 500,000 collective views. I knew these numbers were good, but they were still just numbers. So people were watching my videos . . . then what?

I had plans for the weekend already but they fell through, and I found myself seated in the front row of Devin's workshop. In the hour that followed he opened my eyes to a world I didn't know existed. I thought YouTube was simply a place to share home videos and watch funny cats. According to Devin, it was also a free business space. He described it as a TV network, with specific content and—if used correctly—a steady group of viewers. I could create my own customized channel with my music on my terms. Then Devin taught us how to gain and maintain subscribers and how to use each view to our advantage. It all made so much sense; I couldn't take notes fast enough.

Devin left Utah the following day, but we stayed in touch over the next few months while I started up my own YouTube channel. I harassed him incessantly for pointers until he became one of my best friends and, eventually, my boyfriend.

Dating Devin was a little bit like having a clone. With the exception of playing the violin, he was able to do just about everything I could do. He helped brainstorm ideas, find music video locations, film, and in a pinch he could even help me edit. All the while I did the same for him. We took turns helping each other with projects and then we spent hours sitting on his couch in silence, editing our individual work. It was the perfect system.

At Devin's suggestion, I started my channel by releasing one new video every month. As my popularity grew I started releasing videos more frequently. Since I was trying to work quickly and efficiently,

I did a lot of covers, and one of the first covers that took off was the "Zelda Medley."

It was Devin's idea, and since I had grown up playing a fair amount of video games, I jumped on the opportunity. Devin had done several projects with a composer named Stephen Anderson, so we took my violin solo to him and asked for a full score. At first Stephen thought it was a bad idea to have the violin as the lead, but he worked around my arrangement anyway because he was friends with Devin. Stephen later admitted he didn't think my music would do well, but when it was released, the "Zelda Medley" was one of the most watched videos on YouTube for the week. Since then, Stephen and I have done countless projects together. But he was the first of many people who gave me a chance solely out of respect for Devin.

Up until this point I had a steady four hundred new subscribers a day, but after "Zelda" was released, it went up to two thousand. I kept waiting for the numbers to go back down, but they never did. People were sharing my videos, and for the most part, they liked what they saw! After this boost in confidence I was eager to put out more original music.

When I first started creating my own music I had to pay for all my tracks up front. Now I only pay for a song if I end up using it, but back then there was a lot more pressure to make every beat count. If I didn't like the end result, it was a waste of precious resources. Working in the studio from start to finish usually cost me about two thousand dollars so I couldn't afford to create mediocre tracks. Unfortunately, sometimes I worked on a beat and came home disappointed anyway—which was the case with one of my most popular songs.

When I finished the backtrack for "Crystallize," I hated it. It was overpowering. For months and months I tried to write a violin melody that could hold its own against the dominant backtrack, but they kept ending up in the trash. That's where "Crystallize" was sitting when I found out about some ice castles at a resort in Colorado. They were absolutely stunning, and I was determined to use them in a music video. I got in contact with the creator, Brent Christensen, and offered to make a video to promote his castles if he would pay for my and Devin's flight and hotel accomodations. I guaranteed him at least 400,000 views on my channel with the link back to his website, and he accepted. "Crystallize" was the only finished backtrack I had, so I pulled it out of the trash to give it one more shot. When I finalized the melody I started to like it, but it was unlike anything I had ever written. The dubstep community was either going to love it or tear it to shreds. I prepared a quick rendition of Canon in D (*ew!*) as a backup plan.

From the second we arrived at the ice castles I knew the location was too special to waste on a cover, so I went with my original song. I released "Crystallize" on YouTube a few weeks later, and when it got over one million views in a day I thought the counter was broken. I couldn't believe it. Jennifer had just started working for me, helping to fulfill online orders and sort through e-mails. To make sure I wasn't seeing things, I called and made her double-check the number. She screamed into the receiver, and I screamed back. It was in the top one hundred downloads on iTunes for two days, and it stayed number one on the electronic charts for two months. Immediately, my original music started doing better than my cover videos on YouTube, and I knew this song had changed my life. I hadn't "made it" yet by any means, but I was one step closer and more determined than ever.

Down the road Devin and I went our separate ways. Our reasons for doing so were personal, but in the weeks following the breakup my entire social life crumbled. For eighteen months Devin and I had spent every waking moment chasing our dreams together, working so fast and so hard there was little room for anything, or anyone, else. I knew he was my best friend, but when he was gone, I realized he had become one of my only friends. At the time, I was preparing for my first tour and frantically trying to finish up my debut album before I left. There was so much to be done and so much at stake. Along with feeling lonely I also felt unbearably overwhelmed. Since I began my YouTube channel, Devin had been a part of every major decision I made—encouraging me, supporting me, and picking up the slack when I couldn't do it alone. Suddenly, I had the biggest project of my life on the line, and I was completely beside myself.

Heartache has a way of bringing out the crazy in people. Some wallow, others bury themselves in work, and I got the uncontrollable desire to move. I won't say it was rational, but it was definitely urgent. Within hours of this decision, I had everything I owned packed up in boxes. The act of packing made me feel like I was moving forward with my life, even though I didn't have anywhere to go. I wasn't able to get out of my existing lease, so I lived out of boxes for months, surrounded by cardboard in a hopeless pit of despair. I had invested everything I owned into my tour, and if I didn't produce an album, I knew I would never be able to make the money back. I had two months to write three more songs, design and photograph the album artwork, and make a music video to promote all of the above. The harder I tried to make things happen, the less I accomplished. I was collecting stress like pickles (this analogy would make a lot more sense if you could see my fridge). Then one day I gave up entirely and ate a half-gallon of ice cream, while crying into a pile of dirty clothes. This could have gone on for days had Devin not interrupted me. When I heard him knock on the door, I wiped my eyes and did my best to impersonate someone cheery. He took one look at my forced smile and said, "What's wrong? Have you been crying?"

"No, I'm great."

"What's that in your hair?"

That's when I cracked. I looked at the ends of my hair and tears welled up in my eyes. "It's ice cream," I cried.

Devin had been offering to help me for weeks, and after seeing this spectacle, he insisted. "I'm worried about you. Let me help, please."

"I'm fine, really. It's just been a long day."

"Then do it for me," he persisted. "I want to help."

After everything he had already done for me, asking anything of Devin was too much, but he wouldn't let it go. Over the next few weeks he photographed my album artwork, filmed the "Elements" music video to promote my tour, and was a friend I desperately needed. I know you're all thinking it: why did we ever break up?! I wish we could have stayed together, but some things *are* and some things *aren't*, and our relationship fell into the "aren't" category.

Because I had spent every penny on my upcoming tour, his willingness to photograph and film for free is what made those final touches possible. If it's not already clear, I will spell it out—there would have never been a Lindsey Stirling without a Devin Graham. I guess some people *do* just give people cookies.

THE ITALIAN JOB:
A MUSICAL

The summer after I turned twenty-five, I spent a week performing at a Celtic festival in Courmayeur, Italy. When I was first contacted about participating in the festival I gaped at the e-mail in shock. *Italy? Someone wants to hire me in Italy?* I was still traveling to various college campuses so the thought of going to Europe had me in hysterics. As a kid, I watched the 1995 production of *Riverdance* at my grandmother's house almost every weekend (Michael Flatley, what a babe). I felt as though it had prepared me for this moment in some small way. I pulled myself together long enough to type out a professional-ish response before watching hours of festival footage online.

Prior to my departure, my mom gifted me an undercover security belt she had purchased for her trip to Russia several years earlier. "To carry any valuables," she said, happy to pass along her international travel savvy. What she forgot to mention was how difficult it was to actually access the aforementioned valuables. Every time I had to pay for something, I felt like I was giving a striptease. *You should be tipping me, buddy.* If there's one thing I've since learned from international travel, it's not to draw attention to yourself. Wrestling a giant pouch of money from your bra practically screams, "TOURIST! COME AND GET ME!" I eventually ditched the pouch. After all, I wasn't a tourist; I was a paid musician, a businesswoman, a professional.

When I arrived in Italy, a burly man wearing a dark suit and sunglasses picked me up from the airport in a blacked-out sedan. He did so without speaking a word. His eyebrows resembled two hamsters, and he was wearing at least five pounds of gold jewelry. I was fairly certain he was a Mafioso, hired to murder little American girls. I was trying to devise a plan to retrieve the pocketknife from my secret pouch without being shot, when suddenly we turned a bend and I found myself in the midst of a breathtaking valley, filled with trees and bustling people. After opening the door, my driver reached into a black leather briefcase and pulled out a pair of dancing clogs. He slipped them on and gingerly jumped onto a nearby stage, joining a group of step dancers in rehearsal. Slowly, I retracted my hand from the secret pouch.

"You must be Lin-sey! Welcome to Celtica!" said a voice from behind me.

I turned to see a man in flashy plaid pants approaching.

"My name is Alessandro. I will be your translator for the next few days. Come, you must meet the others!"

Grabbing my violin, I followed him through a clearing toward a giant stage lined with posters—of my face!

"Oh look!" I said. "It's me! Do you have posters for all the acts?"

"No, only the main event," Alessandro said casually.

I stopped in my tracks. "Wait, what?"

He must have seen the shock on my face because he too stopped walking. "Didn't you know?" he asked with a smile. "You are the main attrac-ti-on!" As he said the word *attraction*, he raised up his hands in excitement. "The entire festival was planned around your music."

My previous contact didn't speak fluent English, and it became apparent that a few of the details had gotten lost in translation. I had been under the impression that I was a small act on the bill, but Alessandro and a number of posters now suggested otherwise. I had never headlined anywhere before, let alone a festival! I'm confident I would have fainted, had I not been clenching my butt cheeks together so hard. (I tend to do that when I get nervous; ask anyone who has ever stood behind me at the DMV.)

The following day I got onstage with a dozen Celtic step dancers (including my former driver/hit man) and played in front of six thousand beautiful people. Following the performance I was assigned two security guards to accompany me around the forest grounds. I promptly dismissed them both.

"Thank you, but I will be fine by myself."

No sooner had I left the tent than a group of excited teenagers ran up to meet me, screaming and rattling off in Italian. I smiled and slowly backpedaled into the tent.

"Oh, hey, so I changed my mind. Are those two big guys still here?"

For the remainder of the night I was approached by people of all ages who wanted to shake my hand and take my picture. From every side, hands reached out, waving posters and scraps of the festival program in my face.

"They want your autograph," my security guard said.

When I was in junior high, Miss Arizona spoke about inner beauty at a girls' camp I was attending. Afterward, the other teenage girls and I rushed her for autographs. I didn't know who she was prior to the event, and if you asked me her name today I wouldn't be able to tell you. No matter, at that time, she was the closest thing to a celebrity I had ever encountered. We waited in line and giggled when it was our turn, but the thrill was of the moment. When it was over, I shoved her autographed headshot in my duffel bag, where it probably remains to this day.

As people crowded me at the Festival, I assumed it was much the same. They had seen me perform on the big stage and wanted a memento of the event, not of me specifically. I was their Miss Arizona. But as the night went on I realized something was different. These people were familiar with my videos, they gave me more personalized fan art than I could carry, and many of them had traveled from France, Switzerland, and Poland specifically to see me. It sank in that there were real people behind every click and comment on my channel, and I was staring at some of them. It was one of the best days of my life. But after every high comes a crash.

December 26 is the worst day of the year. The anticipation of Christmas is swept away, taking all the cheery music, colorful lights, and generous people with it. Headlining Celtica was my Christmas, and returning to regular life afterward was December 26. But unlike the holiday, there was no 364-day countdown to my next big opportunity. When I got home, I continued to take any gig I could get, and life returned to normal: working, going to school, and writing music.

A few weeks later I got an offer to play a concert at Webster Hall in New York City. I accepted it the same way I accepted every other gig—immediately and regardless of pay level. Only after I accepted did I realize it was a ticketed show, and I was the only performer of the night. *Whoops, I have got to start reading the fine print.* I had played parties, talent exhibitions, and even a festival, but never completely by myself, and never in a ticketed venue. Italy had proven I had a small following in Europe, but I hadn't the slightest idea if I could draw a crowd in New York City. It was going to be a grand experiment to see if I could sell tickets and put on an entertaining show.

I had recently started working with my first part-time manager. At his suggestion, we decided to use Webster Hall as a showcase to impress potential booking agents in New York. He also insisted I increase the production quality of my performance. In other words, my iPod had to go.

He encouraged me to hire a band, a sound engineer, and a content coordinator. I was completely against it. Paying for their flights, hotel rooms, local transportation, food, music equipment rentals, rehearsal space, and time would cost me a fortune. If I spent the money, I knew I wouldn't be making it back. I protested, loudly, but he was adamant—this was my best chance at landing a booking agent. After much debate, I agreed.

I was introduced to a drummer named Drew, who knew a keyboardist named Gavi, and somehow they both agreed to perform with an electric violinist from YouTube. When it was all said and done, I had spent nearly fifteen thousand dollars. How did I have fifteen thousand dollars at my disposal without a record label, you ask? I wasn't exaggerating when I said I saved every penny from my other gigs to put back into my music. Saving was always the easy part; it was the spending that I struggled with.

On the night of the concert I peeked around the curtain and looked out at a small sea of teenage boys. I'll admit, I was a little surprised by the demographic, but as the lights went down they went wild. Two hundred cracking voices chanted in unison, "Lind-sey! Lind-sey!" Two little syllables never sounded so big.

Gavi cocked his head to listen and then looked back at me with an encouraging smile.

"Who *are* you?"

Drew looked equally shocked. "I thought you said this was your first ticketed show," he said.

Their surprise was nothing compared to mine. "It is," I replied.

As the night went on I realized these people knew more than my name. Every time I introduced an original song they went wild, and every time I referenced one of my videos they roared. I was used to playing in college cafeterias where people were more interested in their coleslaw than my music, but here every eye was on me. I will never forget the sound of the crowd when I took my final bow.

The following morning I got an offer from a booking agent who had attended the show, and within a few months, I had my first small tour scheduled across the United States. Christmas came early, and I've been chasing the paper chain to the next big thing ever since.

THREE

THE PART WHERE I TRY TO TELL ENTERTAINING STORIES ABOUT BEING AN ENTERTAINER

*Of this be sure: You do not find
the happy life . . . you make it.*
—Thomas S. Monson

ALL YOU HAVE
TO DO IS ASK

A vast majority of important and difficult jobs in life are thankless, but I receive endless praise for doing a job I love. It's not fair, and I know that. I feel very lucky. Because of this, it pains me when I can't say *hello* and take pictures with every supportive, adorable, or pleading fan I encounter. I do what I can, but I have to draw the line somewhere. I have to, or else I would become a professional autographer who used to play the violin and tour, but gave it up to make more time for selfies and handshakes. There is a fine balance between how much energy I can give to everyone else and how much I need to reserve for myself.

For me, the definition of personal space is always changing, but there are two places I prefer not to be approached for pictures and autographs: when I am at church and when I am "home." As often as I can, I try to attend Sunday services while I'm on the road. It's the one time I get to slow down, take my mind off work, and worship—which is why I don't sign autographs or take pictures while I'm there. Asking me to be an entertainer in that situation takes me back to the secular world I live in every other minute of the week. Church is a comfortable, spiritual place, and I need that rejuvenation—especially when I'm on tour. Signing autographs in a meetinghouse also makes me feel a little blasphemous. I always love meeting my fans so if you see me at a church near you, please come say hi. Just as long as you remember, it's the Lord's house, not the Lindsey's house.

As for my home, I haven't had anyone show up uninvited to my residence in LA (knock on wood), but my tour manager, Erich, sometimes gets frustrated when fans find and camp out in our hotel lobby. In his mind, they are following me "home." When I am on the road, home is where the cereal is. I always have cereal in the green room, in the hotel room, and on the bus. Other characteristics of my home away from home include space to unpack my things, a lock on the door, and a private bathroom. It's not much, but it is consistent and feels safe. More times than I can count I've gone down to a hotel lobby on the way to breakfast, only to be greeted by excited fans as the elevator doors open. In my mind, I'm walking from my bedroom to my kitchen, but to them I am fair game: *grab her while you can!* I love my fans, but between you and me, I love them even more *after* I've had breakfast.

During my first tour I was taking a nap on the bus when I heard a knock on the door. Assuming one of the guys had forgotten the door code, I opened it to find a wide-eyed preteen boy with curly hair and Coke bottle glasses. When he saw my face he gasped, "Oh! I didn't think you'd answer." Shoving a wad of money in my direction he went on. "Please don't shut the door! All your meet-

and-greet tickets were sold out, but I have seventy-five dollars and I'll pay you the price of a ticket just to talk to you for a minute." My heart melted into a puddle at his feet. I was charging people seventy-five dollars to talk to me—what kind of terrible monster had I become?![2] It's times like these that I am reminded of all the individual people to whom I owe my success. Like this young boy who stood at my bus door with his life's savings, there are thousands of incredible fans all over the world I wish I could thank personally. We had a conversation, and of course I didn't accept his money. But the reason I felt so terrible about his offer was because it came completely out of context. He came to my home (the bus), got me out of bed, and offered to pay me to have a conversation. Had he gone to my place of work (the venue) and offered the woman at the ticket counter the same amount of money to enter the meet-and-greet, his request would have been normal. Meeting fans is part of my job—arguably, the best part of my job—but if I answered the door for everyone that knocked, I would never have a moment to simply be a person. Other times, the situation is a little more dire.

I remember one particularly rough day at the end of my most recent South American tour. I accidentally ate some lettuce in Mexico (which is basically like drinking the water) and my body was not happy. I'll spare you the details, but I got food poisoning . . . and not the good kind. In fact, I spent my last night in Mexico on the floor of my hotel bathroom. The flight home the following day was only two hours, but it may as well have been twenty. I sat in a ball with my knees to my chest the entire time, literally trying to hold myself together. Erich had also eaten the lettuce and was equally afflicted. Finally, with our luggage in hand we exited the airport only to be surrounded by a group of excited fans who grabbed and forcefully pulled me under their armpits for pictures. Erich attempted to step

---

2 Before you start protesting my meet-and-greet ticket prices, keep in mind that it is expensive to cart three buses of people and rented equipment around the country for your viewing pleasure. I love you. Don't judge me!

in, but he was also trying to avoid sudden movement. It was like a horror scene from a movie—where the audience watches something terrible happen, and there's nothing they can do to stop it. Erich and I were the audience to our own tragedy that day. It's an absolute miracle I didn't lose my lunch all over those people. I don't mean to be crude, but sometimes people forget I'm a human, who might have diarrhea and the vomiting reflux of a geyser.

So we're back to the same question: where do I draw the line? It's a day-to-day thing, and I have to continually redefine my personal space based on my needs and the needs of my fans in the moment.

While touring through Mexico City I was walking near the venue when I heard, "There she is!" Looking up, I saw a group of fans sprinting toward me. My first instinct was *RUN!* But midstride I stopped myself. These were my people. Granted, they might trample me or pull me to pieces by accident, but I knew they meant well.

Someday my fans will stop showing up unexpectedly, and I will miss them dearly. So come one, come all! Just please don't push, pull, or force me under your armpit. If you ask me nicely, I'll probably crawl in there on my own.

DO NOT
REPLY

Let's talk self-defense. Everyone knows how to take aim at a testicle, but emotional self-defense is a whole new ball game (see what I did there?). I just wish someone had taught me how to take, or better yet avoid, an emotional beating. Experience has been a good teacher, and now I will pass some of her wisdom on to you. Here's what I've learned in the last few years about emotional self-defense.

STEP 1: ASSESS THE SITUATION (READ THE COMMENTS)

When I first started my YouTube channel, Devin wanted to protect me from the brave anonymous critics in cyberspace. He told me not to read the comments, but I couldn't resist. Had I taken his advice, my ego might still be bigger than a popcorn kernel, and what a tragedy that would be. I consider the comments one of my biggest assets. Reading and responding on my channel is the best way I know to connect with my fans. I value their opinions, I want to hear their feedback, and the best part is, it's free! At the same time, remember to take it all (the good and the bad) with a grain of salt. Which leads me to Step 2.

STEP 2: DO NOT ENGAGE (WITH THE ENEMY)

There will always be people who go beyond constructive criticism to say things that are just plain mean. We call these faceless cyberbullies Internet trolls, and they are constantly searching for an easy fight. Lucky for all of us, the best defense against cyberbullies is to ignore them completely. Their stinging words should only hold as much weight as the adult diaper they are probably wearing so that they never have to leave the computer. When the trolls attack, don't feed them. Delete the comments and move on. If you engage, you run the risk of temporarily turning into a troll yourself, and that is a slippery slope. Even so, it's one thing to delete a comment on the Internet and another to delete it from your mind, which is where your backup comes in.

STEP 3: CALL IN BACKUP

Bring in the troops! Or in my case, call Mom! Your backup doesn't have to be your mom, but make sure it's someone honest, whose opinion you can trust. My mom is my biggest fan and my most reliable critic, so when she tells me I do *not* "dance like a toddler who has to go to the bathroom," I know she is telling the truth.

Apart from nasty comments on the Internet, I have a lot of wonderful supporters who have said things like:

"Lindsey, your a wonderful human bean!!!!"

To that I say, "No, *you* are a wonderful human bean." Here are a few of the many reasons why.

For starters, the people who attend my concerts are anywhere from seven to seventy, and since many of them don't frequent the usual concert scene they break all kinds of stereotypes. They wait patiently, they don't push, they are respectful of the staff and one another, and since many of them are underage, they don't drink or

act sloppy. They come, they wait, they watch, they cheer, and they leave as politely as they arrived. It's beautiful, and wherever I go I know I can count on them to treat one another in a way that would make me proud. In fact, I have fans across the world who have united together in fan groups to support me, and, more important, to support one another. I remember talking with one of these groups in Europe. They were such a close community, and they repeatedly told me how much I had changed their lives. I looked around at all their lovely faces and I knew it wasn't me who had changed their lives—they had changed each other's lives. And while they may not know it, my fans are constantly changing *my* life. Obviously, I could not be a performer without people to support my music. But on a bigger scale, my fans continuously inspire me.

I share a lot of my personal life with the public, and it makes me feel very vulnerable sometimes. When I get letters or hear stories from other people who have overcome their own demons, it gives me strength. On the days when I am tired and discouraged I pull out some of those letters and they remind me why I do what I do. They remind me that there is a bigger purpose to all of this, and that there are wonderful people in the world. These letters remind me that we can help each other.

Some of these people I only get to meet for a few minutes, and thousands of them I've never met at all. But I cherish each one the same. To my fans: You've given me more love and support than I will ever be able to repay. I may not have the chance to respond to every one of you, but I read your letters, I see your comments, and I hear your stories. You are brave, you are strong, and you are beautifully unique. You are the reason I have gotten this far, and you are my motivation to keep going. I love you endlessly, you "wonderful human beans."

LINDSEY GOES WEST:
A TALE OF ONE CITY

Not long ago I was at a restaurant when my server mentioned he was new to the Los Angeles area.

"What brought you out here?" I asked.

He looked embarrassed and replied, "I actually came out here to pursue acting." He motioned toward his apron, forcing a smile. I pulled out a miniature soapbox I keep in my pocket for such occasions and told him there was no shame in working hard to follow his dreams. On the contrary, it was inspiring.

I think that's one of the things I love the most about LA—knowing I can go anywhere and be surrounded by aspiring artists, working hard and following their passions. It's invigorating. Coming to LA alone was one of the first grand voyages I made in my music career, and sometimes I forget how scary it was. You want to hear that story, you say? Okay, I'll tell you.

Following my first show in New York things started happening faster than I was ready for. Before I knew it, I had a full tour booked and was still sitting on an unfinished album. I needed to finish it quickly and professionally, and the only place to do so was Los Angeles. In an act of desperation, my manager reached out to a few people he knew from LA, and at the last minute I got a recording session with a producer named Poet. I was petrified. Up to that point, a close friend and producer in Provo had mastered all the songs on my album. Over the course of a year he and I had worked together whenever I had time and money. It had been a gradual process, and I felt comfortable with the music we created and the way we created it. The thought of walking into a professional studio in LA to play in front of strangers gave me sweaty palms. To make matters worse, my manager called as I was boarding the plane to let me know Poet only had time to record one song. I needed to either convince him to do two or meet someone while I was there to do the last one. He may as well have assigned me the task of growing a second head.

When I arrived Poet was so nice and seemingly buzzed that I actually felt relieved. Maybe he wouldn't notice my mistakes? But the truth of the matter was, by getting into the studio, I had already won the respect of the producer. By taking time to record with me, he had already complimented my work. If only I had realized that at the time, I may not have spent the entire session backpedaling out of timid suggestions.

"Do you think we could add more movement to the chorus? I mean maybe, if you think it's a good idea? I don't know, never mind."

At the end of the first day we had a rough outline for the song, and Poet suggested we record my violin the following morning. It had always taken me several days, if not weeks, to write my violin melodies so I went into Level-10 panic mode. Determined to impress the big-city producer, I stayed up all night creating a violin part. Of course Poet didn't expect me to do that. In fact, when I arrived the next day with a finished melody he was slightly disappointed that I wrote it without him. Oops.

As we were listening to the rough track that night, will.i.am walked through the studio dancing around and high-fiving everyone he passed. When he reached my corner of the room, I did my best to act casual/cool, and we shared an uncoordinated high five, but when all was said and done I had survived my first big LA experience. In case you were wondering, by some miracle I *was* able to grow that second head. While Poet and I were recording I met another producer who had heard "Crystallize," and he agreed to work with me on my final track. I postponed my flight home and spent two days writing and recording the last song on my album, "Zi-Zi's Journey."

I toured supporting my first album for over a year before I moved to LA permanently to begin working on my second. This time I wasn't quite as intimidated by the big-city producers, but it didn't matter. The anxiety over fitting in was replaced by an even more suffocating fear of the sophomore slump (you know, the notoriously horrible second attempt). My first album was largely experimental. I was dipping my toes into the electronic world, releasing one song at a time and taking the feedback as I went. When I started my second album I had a more specific vision in mind. I wanted it to be a concept album about breaking free, specifically from the bonds I had placed on myself. It was much more personal, and the idea that I might fail was much more daunting. I was also worried my first album might have been a fluke—a lucky break. Did I have another one in me? *Yes . . . maybe . . . no . . . I don't know.*

Stress has always been a contributing factor to my eating disorder, and when I started working on my second album it brought out my distorted thinking habits under new guises. Without noticing it I started treating sleep the same way I once treated food—obsessing over it, controlling it, depriving myself of it as an excuse to work harder. When I realized what was happening, I called my own bluff, and then I started doing it with money. My demon is one sneaky devil, but I'm even sneakier. I got a grip (in other words, I called my life coach) and then I went back to work.

When I finally got back into the studio, I was terrified. However, after a full day of work we had the beginnings of my first track. I was getting ready to leave when the producer I was working with set up a mic for my violin.

"Oh, I actually don't write the violin parts in front of anyone," I said politely.

He looked at me quizzically. "That's usually how I do it. Just give it a shot."

Before I knew what was happening, I was in the recording booth huffing and puffing. *Who does he think he is? Pressuring me to play in front of him . . .*

When I stepped out of the sound booth a few hours later I couldn't even remember what I had played. We listened to it a couple times, but I'm always too attached to my music in the moment. I can't tell if I love it or want to throw it across the room. I was still frustrated with the producer for "forcing" me into an uncomfortable situation, so I asked him to e-mail me a copy of the rough track and then I left the studio. I'm slightly embarrassed to admit it, but when I listened to the song a few days later, I started weeping. It was so beautiful! (And I was most likely running on less than four hours of sleep.) But aside from the sleep deprivation and stress, I cried because I knew the song was too beautiful for me to take sole credit for. I felt as if God was hitting me over the head with a rolled-up newspaper saying, "How many times do I have to tell you? I'm not going to make you do this alone!" I sat there listening to the song, choking on my own spit, and I remember thinking, *Why do you care so much about me?* His response was drowned out by the booming chorus of the song. I guess the reasons aren't what's most important. I knew I still had a lot of work ahead of me, but I also knew He was going to help me do it.

BOSS LADY

We've all met that girl—the one who says she only hangs out with guys because other girls are "too dramatic." There's a 96.5 percent chance she is crazier and more dramatic than all the girls she's *not* friends with.

I grew up with sisters, had girlfriends in high school, spent one and a half years with sister missionaries in New York, and lived in an apartment of six girls during college. Then, for my twenty-sixth birthday, I got a tour bus full of dudes. Don't get me wrong, I love my guys, but I was nervous about all the changes in my life. I was starting a new career, with new coworkers, in a new "home," around new friends, in a new city every day. I was a naïve, middle-class white female entering the unknown. And I was coming from Provo, Utah, no less: land of the cardigan-wearing girls named Kelly. Leaving Provo was both thrilling and terrifying. I needed something familiar, *someone* familiar. I was roommates with my close friend Whitney at the time, so when my tour was booked I asked her if she would come out on the road to help with merchandise. And then there were *two* naïve, middle-class white females entering the unknown. I don't know what I would have done without her.

Having Whitney that first year of touring is one of the many ways I've been luckier than I can justify. How did I weasel my way into this rough-and-tumble rock 'n' roll world without getting roughly tumbled? I attribute much of this good fortune to my big hair. While my body might say, "I'm small and vulnerable," my hair warns, "DON'T MESS WITH ME." On a more serious note, the standards I set for myself and my tour have protected me more than anything.

From the beginning, I knew I wanted a clean tour—no drinking during work hours, no alcohol in the green room or on the bus, no stray women in the green room or on the bus, no inappropriate language—you know, the basics. I did not, however, want to be the one to explain these rules to my band and crew. My manager had those conversations. I didn't know how to be the boss—I didn't *want* to be the boss. I wanted to be the boss's cool younger sister, who has some respect but can still join in on a conversation about farts in the back lounge. I think I've finally evolved into that person, but in the transition I spent a period of time as a generic "younger sister," who was neither bosslike nor cool.

My very first opening act was a rapper. Initially he seemed nice enough, but as the days went by he broke every ground rule I had established for the tour. He appeared to be drunk several times, brought random girls back to the bus, and I thought he was vulgar on and off the stage. This made me uncomfortable, but I was inexperienced. I figured his behavior was a by-product of the rock 'n' roll lifestyle. This went on for a week, before I finally confided in my mom how frustrated I was with the situation.

My mom is incredibly respectful of my space and does not get involved in my professional life unless invited. But when I voiced my concerns about my opener she made an exception. As soon as we hung up the phone, she sent an e-mail to my manager that probably went something like this: *Get that man off my daughter's bus, NOW*.

The following morning my manager called and asked me if I had concerns. I simply said, "I don't really want him here anymore, but I can't just ask him to leave." That's when my manager explained to me that actually I could. He was performing on my tour, sleeping on my bus, living on my dime, and breaking my rules. I think that's when it finally sank in: *Oh my gosh, I really am the boss*. A few minutes later my manager called my opener and kicked him off the tour on my behalf. To my surprise, everyone else was relieved to have him gone. I learned an invaluable lesson about leadership, and I was angry with myself for not taking control of the situation sooner. It was up to me to establish the boundaries and to create the environment that I wanted for my work life and my home life—and in my case, the two are often one and the same.

Making bosslike decisions was one thing, but having employees was another. Along with Whitney, Drew, and Gavi, I only had two other crew members—my sound engineer, Rob, and my videographer, Mason. We played six-hundred-seat venues on the high end, and since my tour was small I didn't have an official stage crew. Everyone did a little bit of everything to help out, and I was determined to do the same. A good general is in the trenches, right? For the first several weeks on tour I got up every day with the boys so I could help everyone load in the equipment and set up the stage. I thought they would appreciate the gesture, but I only succeeded in making them all very uncomfortable. On top of getting the stage set up every day, now they had to make sure their little boss didn't get crushed by road cases. Sweating like a brute and getting in everyone's way wasn't helpful, and being a good boss didn't mean I had to do everyone else's job. I've since stopped forcing my help on the guys, but I still try to find little ways to show my appreciation without slowing them down.

My first stage setup. That screen/TV behind me is now in my parents' basement.

My tour family is always growing. At the beginning of a recent tour, I felt really left out and couldn't figure out why the new dancers and crew didn't seem to want me around. They weren't mean, but they sat at separate tables during meals, talked only among themselves, and never invited me when they went places. When I voiced my concerns to Erich he sighed and said, "Lindsey, you're a weird little person."

Not helping, Erich.

He went on. "You're just a different kind of artist. A lot of performers don't know their crew members' names, let alone want to spend time with them. The new hires don't really know where the line is with you."

My tour people are family to me, and in a family there is no line.

I don't need my own lunch table, green room, or bus. What I really need are good people and friends to keep me grounded and help me feel as normal as possible.

It took some getting used to, but being the boss is the best. It means I get final say in everything, and when I'm in my office (bedroom), pants are optional. I think working for me just takes some getting used to, too.

LIVING WITH
BOYS

I met Gavi and Drew the day before my first show at Webster Hall. I was quiet and nervous. I barely spoke to either of them, and when the show was over none of us planned on crossing paths again. Several months later we were all boarding a tour bus, starting what was either going to become my career or just a really expensive road trip.

Touring was new to me, as was living in close quarters with several boys. At first, my elementary school instincts kicked in, and I was determined to fit right in with the guys. On one of our first nights together I started a game of "Would you rather" like so:

"Would you rather have wheels instead of legs that can only run on tracks, or a pickle in place of each arm?"

The guys were kind enough to indulge me for a while, until Gavi asked if he could take a turn. Without hesitation he began, "Would you rather drink a glass of diarrhea once a year for the rest of your life, or dunk your head in a warm porta-potty every month for ten years?"

Immediately the bus erupted in shouts of disgust and laughter. I sat there thinking, *Why didn't anyone laugh when I brought up the pickle arms?* That's when I knew I was living with boys. Oh, how rude of me, allow me to introduce you to my band.

JASON GAVIATI, ON THE KEYS!

Gavi is my work bestie. I know his coffee order, he can tell when I'm upset before I speak, and I've seen him in his underwear more than once (three times to be exact), but we'll come back to that later. We get mistaken for a couple all the time, usually by people on the Interweb who think we look cute together in pictures. I can't argue there, but the reason we have so many pictures together is because we're best friends with a shared addiction to Instagram, not because we're in love. I do love him, though. I love the way he can make anyone feel comfortable and the way he has both literally and figuratively had my back since day one. I love the way his mouth falls open when I share exciting news or break social norms. I love his collection of Brixton hats, his boisterous laugh, and his internal Urban Outfitters homing device.

A few weeks after our first show together I got invited to an event in Portland, Oregon, and was paid enough to hire the band again. Gavi and I were still strangers by all accounts, but we landed in the airport around the same time, so we met up to grab some food. As we ate, Gavi attempted small talk by asking about Devin.

"So, how's your boyfriend? Devin, right?"

"Oh, we broke up." It was still fresh, and I missed the sound of his name. I expected a polite condolence, but without hesitation Gavi lifted his hand for a high five.

"Yeah! Give it here," he said enthusiastically, nearly spitting out his food.

I looked from his outstretched hand to the expression on his face. When I didn't oblige, he lowered his arm.

"Well, I just didn't think you guys were right for each other."

I remember thinking, *Based on what?*

I was offended for all of three seconds, before I replied, "Neither did I, I guess."

And that was the start of my friendship with Gavi—an unreciprocated high five and an unsolicited opinion on my ex-relationship. I met him only three years ago, but enough has happened in those three years to fill thirty; so as far as I'm concerned, I've known him my whole life.

I can only hope I never have to find another keyboard-playing best friend. Those are some big shoes to fill. I would know, since I once tried to wear Gavi's shoes into a venue. It was snowing, and I couldn't find my own. I ended up using one as a toboggan instead.

"I have only spent three years with her, but she already has more
of me than most people I've known my whole life."—Gavi

DREW STEEN, ON THE DRUMS!

Drew knows everything, or at least one random fact about everything. For example: did you know, from all the hospitals around the world, twelve babies go home with the wrong parents every day? Now you do. Along with being my best source of extraneous information, Drew is also one of the most thoughtful members of my tour family. He is always offering to carry my violin or lend a listening ear—and when things go wrong (and they do on a regular basis), Drew is the first person to keep a positive attitude.

In preparation for the Music Box Tour, I had several routines planned around a few projection screens. On the day of our final dress rehearsal, the screens arrived in the wrong size, making the projections I had spent months designing totally useless. I didn't have a backup plan, and with only a few hours of rehearsal left I needed to create one. I took a quick break and went outside to collect my thoughts. *Think, Lindsey. What is Plan B?* After I had been pacing for a few minutes, Drew joined me with a water bottle.

"I thought you might be thirsty," he said, handing it to me. "Don't worry, it's going to be okay. We'll figure something out, we always do."

If I asked Drew to go onstage as one of my backup dancers, I know he would do it. (The boy can do splits without even stretching!) Lucky for him, he's more valuable as a drummer. But it's comforting to know I have so much positive energy behind me onstage every night, and in the venue, and on the bus.

Drew is my band brother and confidant. He does the BEST Valley girl impersonation, and when his hair was long, he used to let me style it from time to time. These are all things I love about Drew. More than anything else, though, I love the look of satisfaction he gets when he is making food for other people.

Drew is a chef in a drummer's body. Given the choice between banging drumsticks and breading drumsticks, I'm not sure which he would prefer. He is the panini maker, the grill master, and the guacamole king. Once, he got sick and went to bed immediately after we finished our set. When the rest of us got back on the bus that night, there was a note on the table directing us to a bowl of fresh guacamole in the fridge. Drew lives to serve other people, and if he were my neighbor in the suburbs, he would be the person I'd call if my lawn mower broke, my cable went out, or I needed a grilled hot dog.

Drew also has some difficult shoes to fill. I once accidentally mistook his Vans for my own, and my feet smelled like a warm garbage disposal for a week.

At first I was worried I would hate touring because I like consistency. I'm actually kind of a homebody. What I didn't know was, apart from the travel, touring is extremely consistent. It's like the movie *Groundhog Day*. I work with the same people every day, eat the same food, and perform the same show. The only thing that makes a week a week is having Sundays off. Other than that, it's just a bunch of days in a row, which are nearly identical in structure. I love it. What I should have been worried about is the limited personal space, which has resulted in the occasional underwear run-in.

The first time I walked in on Gavi dressing, I stared. Yeah, his tush is nice and all, but I was more surprised than anything. I was looking for my computer case and walked into the green room to find Gavi bent over, pulling on his pants. All the lights were off, and he was facing the opposite corner. As I opened the door, a beam of light landed right on his bum. It was a little magical, but mostly weird. He turned to look at his intruder, and I was so surprised that I just stood there for a good two seconds—one Mississippi, two Mississippi. That's a long time when you're staring at someone in their underwear! Finally, Gavi said, "Uhh, leave."

"Oh, right."

I looked down and closed the door. Later that night, Gavi announced to everyone that I stared at him in his underwear.

"She opened the door and just stood there!"

"I was surprised!"

"I had to tell her to leave!"

"Well, you need to lock the door."

Another time I walked into the back lounge of the bus looking for my makeup and stumbled on a similar sight, except this time I closed the door more quickly. It happened a third time one night before a show in Paris. I ran into the office to get my violin strings and there he was, in his bent-over underwear stance.

"Are you serious?!" he yelled.

"Stop changing where my stuff is. And lock the door for once!" I yelled back.

In his defense, sometimes there aren't locks. To avoid being seen in my skivvies, I sing what I call "The Changing Song." Which is really just me yelling, "I'm changing in the back lounge!" over and over again.

The tune changes according to my mood, and it warns off any males who might otherwise come wandering in. In the case that someone isn't paying attention to my song and tries to open the door anyway, I resort to letting out a loud shriek, and that usually causes the door to slam shut very quickly. (In case you were wondering, Gavi is a tiger-print underwear kind of guy.)

Once, during a meet-and-greet in Germany, one of my fans reached behind me like he was going to give me a hug and then picked me up by my butt—a double-fisted cheek grab. I didn't appreciate it much, and Erich was mortified that it happened on his watch. The next day at the meet-and-greet he was on high alert. Before the evening started, he called a special meeting with the venue security. I was not to be picked up under *any* circumstances. About halfway through the meet-and-greet, a lanky, middle-aged man ran toward me with uncontained excitement. I saw him coming in slow motion, arms outstretched, body bending slightly to pick me up. Before I could warn him against it I was cradled in his arms. I remember thinking, *You really don't want to do this*, but it was too late. Erich, Gavi, Drew, my male dancers, and three German security guards all shouted in unison and ran toward us, as if I was a Ming vase that had been hurled across the room.

"No no no!"

"Put her down!"

"STOP!!!"

The man was absolutely harmless, but he put me down so fast I nearly lost consciousness. I did my best to console him that "Really, it's okay," and we laughed uncomfortably together, each of us equally red in the face. *Take it down a notch, boys!*

I often get asked if and when I'm going to get a bodyguard. The thing is, I already feel like I've got several—and as long as Drew and Gavi are around, I'll always have at least two. Navigating the ins and outs of the entertainment industry without a clue was over-whelming, but these guys have been with me from the beginning. I can't say that about anyone else. The fact that they are still setting sail on new adventures with me is almost too good to be true. I keep waiting for the other shoe to drop. When it does, I really hope it isn't as gigantic as Gavi's or as smelly as Drew's.

THE DIFFERENCE BETWEEN
DREW AND GAVI

On one of our days off, we found a karaoke bar near our hotel and made plans to go later that night. A few hours before we were supposed to meet up, I walked past Gavi's hotel room and overheard him practicing Backstreet Boys songs.

"Quit playing games with my heart!"

That night, Gavi murdered his song onstage.

Drew, on the other hand, slept right up until it was time to go and purposely picked the worst song for his vocal range: "Take On Me," which murdered *him* onstage.

YOU'LL THANK ME WHEN
YOU'RE OLDER

Writing about Erich has been impossible. Like watching a 3D movie from the front row—it all seems too up close and personal. The world could collapse into the ocean, and Erich would know what to do about it. There has never been a situation he couldn't fix, and sometimes I worry he's actually a robot created by the Russian Mafia to get the inside scoop on YouTube . . . or smiling. See what I mean?! I'm trying to write a simple intro, and it's falling to pieces! If I had to describe our relationship in one sentence it would be this: "I've never been embarrassed of you, but I have been embarrassed *for* you, several times."

Those were his words, not mine.

When Erich came on as my TM (tour manager), it was supposed

to be temporary. The TM I originally hired had a family emergency right before the tour, and Erich was called in as a sub. It was a short gig, two weeks max. Those two weeks turned into two years, and I hope those two years are a preview for the next two decades.

For several years I was the only girl on my tour. As a result, I got a lot of extra attention. Even now, someone is always offering to carry my bag, open my door, or give up their window seat on planes. I like to think it's because I'm such a classy lady, not because I'm their boss. As nice as all that is, being the only female on the road has a few disadvantages as well. Namely, I don't have anyone to borrow tampons from in a pinch. I've had to ask Erich to send out a runner for feminine products more often than I would like to admit. I can multitask like nobody's business, but ask me to re-member when my period will come, and I draw a blank. When my "monthly diva" arrives, I find myself surrounded by a bunch of dudes who try to stay out of my way but end up aggravating me no matter what. *Can everyone just admit that I'm right? About everything!*

I remember going to a show in Park City, Utah, when my monthly diva was visiting. I hadn't seen Erich in a few weeks, but when I got to the venue, I blew past his office and went straight to my dressing room. When I tried on my costumes a few minutes later, none of them fit correctly—bunching where there shouldn't be bunches and pinching in places I didn't appreciate.

I was moody.

I was bloated.

I complained about my costumes.

I didn't say hi to Erich.

Later, I found out Erich was ready to stage an intervention, be-cause, as he put it, I had finally "gone all Hollywood."

Just a few days later I was sitting in my dressing room with Drew, Gavi, and Erich, feeling proud of myself.

"Guys, I have to say, I recently went through my 'lady time,' and I think I handled it very well. I bet none of you even noticed!"

Gavi scoffed, and Drew tried to nod convincingly.

"That explains a lot," Erich said with a visible sigh of relief.

I couldn't believe it! I thought I had been so coy. Since then, Erich has started using the My Monthly Cycles app, so he can keep track of my mood and "avoid unnecessary judgment," as he says. However, if there ever comes a time when my entitled behavior doesn't line up with Erich's schedule, I made him promise to sit me down and bring me back to reality. I don't belong in Hollywood.

As TM, Erich is also very protective of my time and energy. Sometimes I try to pack too much into one day, and Erich is frequently the voice of reason that says, "Slow down." When I don't listen and end up getting sick, Erich is also the one who makes sure I drink water, eat regularly, and go to bed at a decent hour. He's like my dad, only he doesn't wear a scarf or a hat; and he has more tattoos. In fact, he frequently tells me I remind him of his daughter. I never know if that's a compliment or not: *Does he love me like a daughter, or am I acting like a twelve-year-old?*

I've come to realize it's almost always the latter. For instance, one night after a show we had plans to meet a promoter for dinner. I got off the bus wearing cutoff sweats and a T-shirt.

Erich saw me and asked, "Are you really wearing that?"

I looked down at my clothes and replied, "Um, yes?"

"No, no you can't. Go change."

"But I just played a two-hour show. I want to be comfortable."

"Be comfortable in something that doesn't make you look homeless."

Ugh, Dad!

Following these disagreements, he always gives me a look that says, *You'll thank me when you're older.* Other dadlike things Erich says on the regular include:

- "Do you want to brush your hair a little before we leave?"
- "Where are your shoes?"

- "Please don't go on stage wearing that."
- "Leggings aren't pants."
- "Did you eat lunch?"
- "I see you have a crush on _____."

On a more serious note, a few tours ago I found myself in a rut, struggling with some resurfacing eating disorder habits. Erich noticed I hadn't been myself, so he reached out to Brooke and asked her for any advice on how to make things easier for me. She gave him a few suggestions, and shortly after, all the scales disappeared from my hotel rooms, replaced by a variety of my favorite snacks. Stealing my scales and arranging for special groceries is not part of Erich's job description. His duties include—but are not limited to—advancing my tour, coordinating with venues, arranging transportation and accommodations, tour accounting, troubleshooting, and scheduling press. But Erich has always been so much more than a tour manager to me. He put it best in a letter when he wrote: "I don't know whether to write this to a coworker, daughter, sister, boss, or friend."

If I had to choose one, I'd say daughter. No . . . sister— no . . . friend. Oh, forget it.

HOW TO FIND
ME IN A CLUB

When I was younger I thought the best way to get a guy's attention was to run faster or throw harder than anyone else. Most girls learn early on that this flirtation method doesn't work and they try something else—like being dainty and delicate. I've tried being dainty and delicate, but I'm better at being me. If you want to find me in a club, look for the sexiest girl in the room. Then turn slightly to the left, and you will see me dancing much faster and harder than her.

TRAVEL PANTS

In college, I took a road trip with a guy friend of mine and his younger sister. Being the classy gentleman that he was, he came to my door to help carry my luggage. At the sight of me in my pajamas he asked, "Why aren't you dressed yet?" For a moment I panicked and thought I had forgotten to put on pants again. Glancing down, I heaved a sigh of relief and then looked back at him in confusion. "I am dressed. This is what I'm wearing."

"That?" he asked, pointing at my T-shirt and baggy drawstring pants.

Now I was annoyed. "Yes, Jack, you will have to share the car with me and these apparently repulsive pajama pants for the next eight hours."

"Okay, okay," he said, surrendering with his hands. "I was just checking."

I have good reason for traveling like a nine-year-old at a slumber party. First of all, I want to be comfortable enough to fall asleep in the car or on the plane. I don't put on unnecessary makeup (because sleeping in makeup makes me feel gross) and if my hair isn't done, I don't have to worry about ruining it. See? All good reasons.

Once Jack and I got to the car I realized why he had been so apprehensive. In the front seat sat his sister, and from where I was standing I could see she had curled her hair. It was the first tip-off that something wasn't right. When she turned to wave at me, I nearly dropped my bag in horror. *Ah!* Her makeup was flawless, she wore a dainty scarf, and she even had on earrings. Who was she trying to impress, anyway? The guy in the front seat was her *brother*. Then I realized it was me—she was trying to impress me. Why do girls do that? All she had to do was bring a pair of regular shoes and she would have one-upped my slip-on sneakers (which are so comfortable, by the way).

The more I travel, the more I've come to realize that the average female treats a travel day the same as any other—by getting dressed, putting on makeup, and doing her hair. The introduction of yoga pants into mainstream society has made my travel attire slightly more acceptable, but I still get ready for a long flight the same way I get ready for bed—by washing my face, pulling my hair back, and putting on my pajamas.

Once, I was at an event where another performer went off on

a rant about how tacky it is when people show up to the airport in sweats, or worse, pajamas.

I remember feeling slightly defensive for myself and all the other people who were following my trendsetting example.

"Maybe they want to sleep on the plane because that's the only sleep they're going to get that day," I said casually.

"But pajamas? Really? There are other ways."

"I can't sleep in jeans!" I blurted.

She looked confused, and I slowly backed out of the room.

Recently, I added leg weights to my travel look. There was a period of time when I had fly dates almost every other day. My tour was traveling through Asia and South America, and I felt like I was living in the airport. To keep myself from going insane, I wanted to find some good ways to multitask en route. Since I was trying to get in shape for my tour, I bought a set of leg weights— you know, the giant hacky sacks that strap to your calves. I walked around in them all day, and while we waited in long lines I did exercises that made my crew roll their eyes and turn their backs. Once, I grabbed Gavi's arm for balance during my leg lifts, and he said, "Please don't touch me right now, people will think we're together."

"But we are together. I'm your boss."

"Don't remind me."

None of the guys were very fond of my public exercise routine, but no one hated my leg weights with more conviction than Erich. Every time I put them on, he knew there was a fifty-fifty chance he would have to argue with an airport security employee before boarding the plane. The weights have metal inserts in them, and for obvious reasons they aren't very popular among the security staff. For months, we said they were doctor-prescribed for therapeutic reasons, and it worked. Until one day in Brazil, a security worker put his foot down.

"You cannot wear those onto the plane, they are too heavy."

"But even with the leg weights, I still weigh less than all these guys," I said, pointing at my crew.

He folded his arms across his chest, and I knew it was game over. Reluctantly, I unstrapped my weights and said a bitter good-bye before leaving them behind. A few weeks later, Erich and his wife gifted me a new set under one condition: I was not allowed to wear them through airport security. I still love my weights, but they have been reserved for press days and tourist activities.

Airline companies are pretty unaccommodating in general, but hundreds of hours spent in airports across the world have given me some insight into the battles that are worth fighting, and which ones are better left alone. The leg weights had a good run, but getting two steel-plated contraptions through a metal detector might have been asking a little much. I'm actually surprised they lasted as long as they did. Understandably, airports have a strict set of rules to follow. Regardless, I feel like they overuse specific phrases for convenience's sake. Some of their favorites include, "There's nothing we can do," or "It's government regulation."

I've heard it said before that once the plane door is closed, no one gets on—government regulation, there's nothing they can do about it. Once, I watched a woman with a stroller run up to the gate moments after they had closed the plane door.

"I'm sorry, ma'am, the plane door has been closed. There's nothing we can do."

Not long after, I found myself in the same situation, sans the stroller.

"You closed it early!" I whimpered as I ran up to the gate. The airline worker shook her head.

"I'm sorry," she said.

I held up my ID with a frown. "But it's my birthday . . ."

She stared back at my desperate face and said, "Oh, okay," and she opened the door! *But what about government regulations?* I half expected Air Force One to show up and reprimand both of us. I guess the phrase "nothing we can do" is relative when it comes to TSA policies. If there is one thing that really is out of their control, though, it's the use of passports for international travel.

They say depression is the leading cause of anxiety, but I would beg to differ. Passports are the real culprits. They are so small and so important. Without one, you are literally no one, from nowhere! No matter how many times I've checked to make sure I have my passport, every time Erich asks for it my heart drops. I honestly feel like there is a ten percent chance it came to life and walked away. In 2014, we did a US tour that spilled into Canada a few times, and the day before we left for Vancouver, I realized I forgot my passport in California. Brooke was working for me at the time, and minutes after this realization she came into the room to admit she had forgotten her passport as well. Leave it to the Stirling girls. Erich made some phone calls before he confirmed that really, there was nothing he could do. We couldn't return to the US without a passport, so leaving without one was out of the question. That night, my bus dropped Brooke and me off at a hotel. Everyone else continued on the road without us, so they could get all the equipment to Vancouver on time. Then, one of the assistants from my management office in California got on a plane with my passport, handed it to me in the Seattle airport, and flew right back to work. (Sorry, Casey!) There was no way around it, and I can respect that. But not every situation is so black-and-white.

When I was working on my second album, I found myself on the verge of an emotional breakdown. My manager insisted I take a break, so I threw a few things into a bag and booked a red-eye home to see my parents. Ten minutes before my flight was scheduled to board, it got canceled. I had already been crying, so with running mascara and puffy eyes, I walked to the counter and asked if I could get a hotel room.

"I'm sorry, ma'am, we've already used up our quota of hotel vouchers for the day. I wish I could help, but there's nothing I can do."

I don't usually play this game, but in that moment I knew the difference between the "nothing" she was referring to and the "nothing" that really means nothing. The airport could take my leg weights, and they could hold me hostage without a passport, but in my current emotional state they were not going to deny me a hotel room. I looked at her with my tear-soaked eyes, and then with a forced calm in my voice, I said slowly, "I really need a hotel room." She stared at me for a moment. Then she held up an index finger, gesturing for me to wait, and picked up the phone.

"Yes, we have a four-two-two, I need a quota override," she said into the receiver.

I'm pretty sure that's code for, "We have a crazy person on our hands. Can I use one of the super-secret hotel vouchers?"

She hung up and said calmly, "All right, Miss Stirling, we will get you a room for the night."

The way she spoke made me wonder if the room she had in mind was padded, but at that point, I didn't even care. My approach was a little unhinged, but it was the best I could do in the moment, and I think she understood that. Bless her.

Don't get me wrong, I think rules are important. Most of the time, they are there for our safety or public order, yada yada; but I also think sometimes it's okay to ask for an exception. Unless we're talking about travel attire, in which case it's always okay to be the exception. Travel pants are better than no pants at all. At least that's what I've always said.

FLIGHT
ETIQUETTE

Sometimes I feel like the airport is my second home. On our last tour through Australia, Asia, and South America, my team took fifty-five flights in two months. It's the less glamorous side of the rock 'n' roll lifestyle. Yes, I get to do what I love. But a few hours later we're all sleeping on suitcases in front of an airport gate, waiting for our turn, like everyone else. If I had a quarter for every time I've tried to squeeze my body beneath the metal armrests by the gate I could buy my own jet.

Having spent so much time in the air, I can say with confidence that a long flight is only as good as the people around you. Sitting by someone with bad flight etiquette is like moving into a new house and finding out your neighbor is a serial sex offender. I know, I'm being a little dramatic. Having a sex offender for a neighbor isn't quite as bad as sitting by an inconsiderate flyer, but you get the idea.

Here are the types of flyers you will want to avoid, and if you can't avoid them, at least avoid becoming one of them.

THE SECURITY LINE STOPPER

I give you the reason we all have to arrive two to three hours early for a flight. I'm usually behind this person in the security line—the one who accidentally leaves their laptop in their laptop bag, forgets to take their shoes off, is carrying an open water bottle, and tries to go through the metal detector with a switchblade in their pocket. When I'm in a hurry, part of me feels like helping this person. The other, more assertive part of me would like to push them onto the luggage conveyor belt and get it over with.

THE BIN HOGGER

I think we've all witnessed this one—the person who is trying to wrestle a gigantic carry-on into the overhead bin. Not only is it a little bit selfish to take up that much space, it's also uncomfortable to watch. If you haven't witnessed this spectacle yet, here's a short recap of what it looks like: Man lifts giant bag toward tiny overhead bin. Giant bag falls backward on man's face. Flight attendant tells man his bag won't fit. Man is convinced it will fit if he grunts harder while pushing. Man's shirt comes untucked during the scuffle, and his hairy belly button is now exposed. It's a lose-lose for everyone.

THE SCREEN PUNCHER

Most planes have nifty touch screens on the back of every seat. Modern technology is really great. What's not really great is when the person behind you has never used a cell phone, tablet, or ATM, and attacks every button like a game of Whac-A-Mole. The touch screen is not a punching bag; it's the back of someone else's pillow.

THE SEAT GRABBER

This is the person who thinks the seat in front of them is a handrail and uses it to hoist himself or herself up several times throughout the flight. This causes a jolting sensation for the person sitting on the other side of the handrail, because it's not actually a handrail at all. It's a seat—most likely one that someone is trying to sleep in.

THE ELBOW RESTER

Unless you are sitting in an aisle seat, you should share your armrests. You only paid for half, so don't take up the whole thing—even if your arm is bigger, heavier, or more selfish than your neighbor's.

THE TALKER

Guilty as charged! I'm the talker. I really enjoy conversing with strangers, but I think I'm pretty good at reading basic body language. Here are some common "I don't want to talk right now" signs to look for. If you notice someone doing any of the following, it's time to zip your lips:

- fiddling with their headphones
- trying to avoid eye contact
- grabbing a book or magazine
- glaring at you
- squeezing their eyes shut

Every now and again, I'm on the other side of the looking glass. When I need a little shut-eye, I use the above signals (minus the glaring), and if all else fails, my go-to is an original I like to call "the codfish face"—eyes closed, head back, mouth open. Works every time.

THE COST

In the dream I was at a party. I saw my roommates, a few people from church, and a woman with curly red hair. She wore a long, dark jacket that wrapped easily around her thin frame, making her look like a secret worth keeping. It was a crowded party, but she stared at me as if we were the only two people in the room. I can still picture her now—eyes narrow, lips pursed.

In an attempt to ignore her gaze I tried to engage in conversation with other people, but my presence was invisible to everyone, except for her. As I was about to leave, I looked up to see her standing right in front of me. She smiled, and I saw the devil in her squinty eyes. A cold chill ran up my spine and I knew I couldn't leave. Around us people laughed and played games, but all I could focus on was the woman in the long jacket and the fear in my chest. When she walked away I followed her involuntarily into the kitchen where she placed a contract in front of me, pricked my finger with a needlelike fingernail, and told me to sign it with my blood. Every time I wanted to do anything, a new contract appeared. I wanted to sit down—she handed me a contract. I wanted to wash my hands— she handed me a contract. I wanted to check my phone—she handed me a contract. As frightened as I was, the thought of trying to leave was always more terrifying, so I signed all her contracts and remained in her control for what felt like hours.

Finally, I felt her power over me lessen and I was able to escape. I sprinted back to my apartment, slammed the door, and fumbled with the knob, but the lock was gone. In desperation, I turned and ran toward my room, but was stopped short by the sight of Brooke in the living room. She was tied to a chair in front of our large glass window. When I lunged to untie her, she spoke calmly.

"DON'T. If you untie me, she will know. If you do anything, she will know."

Her wrists were raw from the tight cords of rope.

I woke up trembling. Lingering in my mind were the memories of Brooke's bloody hands and the face of the evil woman. I was home alone, and for the next hour I was afraid to leave my bedroom. So I retraced the steps of my dream, over and over again. I knew the woman represented my eating disorder—I understood her control over me—but I couldn't understand why Brooke was involved. It haunted me.

A few hours later Brooke returned home from her morning shift at a nearby barn. Her hair was in a messy bun, the smell of wood shavings on her clothes. As she removed her dirty jeans and pulled on a fresh pair, I told her about the dream and the woman in the long jacket. I talked while she brushed her hair into a ponytail, buttoned up her jacket, and pulled on a pair of rain boots. When I finished, she looked at my reflection in the closet mirror and said, "What a strange dream. We're out of toothpaste and shampoo. Can you think of anything else I should pick up?"

I shook my head. I hadn't even gotten out of bed yet.

Then she walked down the hall, past the large glass window, and out the door.

A few years later, Brooke moved back to Arizona to get married and I was prepping for my first tour. Out of the blue she called me and broke down on the phone.

"I forgive you," she said. "I just need to tell you I forgive you."

I was confused. Our last conversation had been about my latest awkward date and the best shade of sea-foam green for her wedding.

"What do you mean? . . . Did I do something that upset you?" I asked carefully.

"I forgive you." She paused to steady her voice. "For your eating disorder. For what it did to you, for what it did to me, for what it did to our relationship."

"Brooke, I didn't know . . . I don't understand."

"I know you've noticed that we aren't as close as we once were, and I know you don't understand why, but it changed you. It changed us."

I heard what she was saying, but it still hadn't sunk in.

"I'm so sorry," I said, "but I still don't understand. How did my eating disorder affect *you*?"

She sniffed, and I imagined one of her tears falling onto the receiver, inky with mascara.

"Every time Mom called, I felt like it was to see how *you* were doing—I knew she cared about me, too, but I couldn't talk to her about my problems when she was already so worried about yours. And when you cried because you didn't feel like you fit in with our new roommates, I wanted to tell you it was because you couldn't connect with *anyone* anymore, but instead I listened and tried to make you feel better. Or when I wanted to go out for ice cream or hot chocolate, you went running instead. And when I finally convinced you to come out to eat with friends, I saw the way you focused on picking around the cheese in your salad instead of joining the conversation or listening to anything I had to say. And when we got home, I always got to hear about how fat and bloated you felt—and it was I who constantly had to convince you it wasn't true.

Even when you stopped complaining about it out loud, I noticed the look in your eye when you turned sideways to look at your stomach in the mirror instead of my face when I talked. You stopped being my sister, and you didn't care about anything besides your body, and I've been so angry at you for it."

After a pause, Brooke spoke again.

"I don't want you to feel bad. Please don't be sad. I know I played my own part in all of this, too . . ."

"I didn't know . . ."

"I needed to tell you so that we can move on. So we can get back to where we used to be. I want to be sisters again."

The line went still and I felt dizzy. Could this really be true? I had spent the last few years healing on my own, and it had never occurred to me to say sorry to anyone else. In a matter of moments, my mind reeled from shock to devastation. How selfish I had been, assuming my problems were mine alone. The fact that I never knew to ask forgiveness was almost as painful as the fact that I had hurt her in the first place. This was why we weren't friends anymore. *I* was why we weren't friends anymore. And then my mind drifted back a few years, and I remembered the woman wrapped in black from my dream, the needlelike point of her finger, and Brooke tied up by the window. We hung up the phone, and I cried. I had made my sister a captive to my own problems.

Following the phone call we both tried to start over, but it was difficult to do from opposite sides of the country, or different countries altogether. It wasn't natural. It felt like we didn't have anything in common anymore, and when we talked it was stale. After a year of obligatory phone calls and "how are yous," I found out Whitney wouldn't be coming back on tour, and in a spur-of-the-moment decision I asked Brooke if she would come out on the road with me for a few weeks. When she said yes, I was surprised. Our relationship was still awkward, and the thought of spending three weeks in close quarters with her made me nervous.

While on tour, Brooke found small tasks here and there to help with, but her most important job was to be my sister. We stayed up at night talking, our similar sense of humor resurfaced, and she became my constant companion. We started sharing things again—clothes, food, a bus, friends, hotel rooms, jokes—and every night she stood side-stage and jumped up and down throughout the entire set. We also found a pear that looked like it had a butt crack, so we drew low-rise jeans on it and left it around the bus to moon people. You know, sister stuff.

On the night before she left, I purposely scared her as she came out of the bathroom. She jumped forward, stumbled over my luggage, and face-planted violently into the floor. We belly-laughed for what felt like hours, making up for some of the years we had lost.

The next morning, I found the following letter on my suitcase:

Lindsey,

The thought of leaving has had me on the verge of tears for the last few days—these three weeks have been some of the best of my entire life. I wasn't sure what to expect when I came out here. I was nervous, but it has been better than I could have ever imagined. I feel so blessed to have been able to be here, to be part of your new life, and to meet all the wonderful people you have on your team; but more than anything I feel like we are finally sisters again. When I left BYU our relationship wasn't where I wanted it to be, and although we've both made some changes, we never quite got the opportunity to put it back together. This is the first time I have "lived" with you since then, and I can finally say we are as close as we used to be—probably closer than ever. It has been an experience I will never forget.

When I get home I know I will wish I was on the road with you again, but being sad means these memories are worth missing. I can't thank you enough for sharing your time, your money, and your friends. I'm so sad I won't be there to see your biggest show, but I know there will be more where that came from in the future. If you ever need a roadie again, you know where to find me.[3]

Keep chasing rainbows girl, you're going to catch them all.

Love you infinity,
Brooke

When I finished the letter, I cried—not because she was gone, but because she was back.

---

3 The following summer I brought Brooke out with me on my entire US tour. When I got extremely homesick the following year in Asia, my management flew Brooke out to bring me a piece of home. I found her in my Tokyo hotel room—wearing every article of clothing from my suitcase. You know, sister stuff.

Day off in Orlando, Florida. She's wearing my shirt, I'm wearing her pants.

FALLING IN LOVE
IS HARD TO DO

I think one of the biggest challenges we all face is falling in love . . . with ourselves. In junior high, all the popular girls had chunky blond highlights and golden-brown skin that glistened while they talked with boys in the courtyard. I had dirty-brown hair and the Irish pallor of my forefathers. My mom didn't want me to color my hair yet, but I heard it from a reliable source that lemon juice would bring out my natural highlights. I was also told that olive oil would accentuate a healthy glow in my skin. I lathered myself in these liquids, head to toe, and literally baked in the sun for several hours. When I was finished, I walked away with the same brown hair as before. My skin, on the other hand, now had the healthy glow of a ripe tomato. Given that I was essentially wearing the ingredients for vinaigrette, I had made myself into a caprese salad.

Not long after, "scrunching" hair was the thing to do. If I couldn't have blond hair, maybe I could at least make it wavy. The secret formula? Eggs. I slapped a few egg whites on my scalp and scrunched for several minutes until my hair was a very stringy (but still straight) mess. Even recently I went for a more official treatment to help control the frizz in my hair—a Brazilian blowout. Word on the street is it works for everyone . . . except me. My hair was just as frizzy, only after the blowout, it was also extremely flat.

When it comes to appearances, I believe we can all find things to love about the things we don't like. For instance:

1 I love my full-scale horse teeth because I got them from my dad.
2 I love my hairy arms because brushing them calms me.
3 I love my small boobs because they don't pummel me in the face when I dance.
4 I love my stubby fingernails because they don't get in my way when I play my violin fast.
5 I love that my hair won't grow much past my shoulders because . . . I just do.
6 I love my four recurring chin whiskers because I've named them "the Whisky Bros," and they're like a loyal gang of friends.
7 I love my acne-prone skin because it reminds me of my youth.
8 I love my hairy knuckles because they collect pollen and help support the ecosystem.

I love myself.

See, that wasn't so hard. Now it's your turn.

1 I love my _____ because _____

2 I love my _____ because _____

3 I love my _____ because _____

4 I love my _____ because _____

5 I love my _____ because _____

6 I love my _____ because _____

7 I love my _____ because _____

8 I love my _____ because _____

I love myself.

As you should! Don't let the bad guy tell you otherwise. Looks aside, the battle to fall in love with ourselves starts much deeper than the surface. I was on a panel for an "Empowering Women" event, when someone from the audience asked how she could feel more comfortable in her skin. One of the other speakers responded, "You just have to be confident, you have to own yourself!" I liked where she was going, but I felt like her answer was a little lacking. You can't simply tell an insecure person to be confident, the same way you can't tell a depressed person to be happy, or a slow person to be fast. I wish it were that easy, but there are steps to every process. I've tried to will myself to be the things I want to be. *Pull yourself together, Lindsey. Be happy. Be confident!* It might work momentarily, but without anything to support it, this kind of approach is exhausting. It's like doing a sprint when you're out of shape— you'll crawl to the finish line and never want to run again. I've since learned that positive thinking and confidence are muscles that need continuous work and attention. I exercise these muscles by meditating, eating properly, talking to a life coach once a month, listening to motivational speeches, and starting my days with scripture study. Do I always succeed? No. Am I always happy? Of course not. But I'm working on it, and that's all anyone can do.

As someone who has lost every shred of confidence multiple times, I've had to rediscover myself more than once. Every time, I learn something new. I've learned that I don't like asking for help, I'm afraid of being a disappointment, I rely too heavily on positive feedback, I have a habit of comparing myself to others, I use work to run from my emotions, and I worry I will literally become invisible

(I never claimed I was always rational). I've also learned I have the ability to change and that I can become the kind of person I admire. But it takes practice.

It comes as no surprise to me that a prima ballerina has put in hours upon hours of practice. And yet, I see a mother of four with the patience of Job, and I assume she was born with it. She wasn't born with it any more than that Maybelline model was born with dark eyeliner and perfectly angled eyebrows! That model practiced long and hard to get those brows right, and that mom is patient because she works at it, not because she's perfect. I'm so far from perfect I couldn't touch it with a ten-foot pole. Luckily I don't need to be perfect. I just want to do my best and love myself in spite of my imperfections. I want that for you, too.

A MESSAGE
FROM PHELBA

I'd like you to meet Phelba, my number one fan. She came into existence one day in New York when I was only a few tickets shy of a sold-out show. Tired of the constant self-promotion, I decided to let someone else take a turn. That day, *she* went out on the town and told as many people as possible about Lindsey Stirling. She's basically the ten-year-old version of myself—socially awkward, bold, and uninhibited. Since that day in New York, she has followed me around the country trying to promote my music and meet me face-to-face. We've never met, and we never will, but I know I can always count on her to love and support me, no matter what. She is shameless, pathetic, and nearly impossible to dislike. It would be like hating a puppy with three legs. I've included a letter she wrote below.

Dearest Lindsey,

I'd like to apologize for our earlier misunderstandings, and don't worry, I'm no longer upset about the restraining order. Sometimes ya just gotta be the bigger woman. Anywho, I hear you are writing an autobibliography, and as your #1 fan I feel it is my responsibility and due diligence to lighten the load. So please feel free to include the following with proper citation:

Hello all Secondary Fans,

If you're reading this, it's official—I am better than you. For any of you pickle-brains out there who don't know who I am, my name is Phelba. That's spelled P-H-E-L-B-A. Most people refer to me as Queen of the Stirlingites, aka Lindsey's #1 fan. Here are the reasons why:

First of all, I'm practically Lindsey's understudy. Do I play the violin? Absolutely not. But do I know every step of choreotography? You bet your Benjamins I do. I could jump onstage and perform in a moment's notice. Put me in, coach! Secondly, I'm responsible for over half of Lindsey's YouTube views. 503,455,012 views to be exact. Yes I've counted, haven't you? No you haven't, BECAUSE YOU'RE NOT A NUMBER ONE FAN! Thirdsies, I only wear Lindsey Stirling Merchandise. By the way, if you buy a T-shirt four sizes too big and tie a shoelace around the middle, it becomes a dress. I wear mine to weddings and churchy stuff. It's a huge hit and people are always staring. Fourthish, I know where Lindsey is at all times. I bet you'd like to know how I know . . . I'll never tell. Fifthly, all the security staff at the venues know me by face, name, and fingerprint. And Last but not least, I heard it from someone somewhere that Gavi thinks I'm hott. Don't make me say it again, I'm blushing so hard right now.

So to anyone reading this, I think it's clear that you're not cut out to be a #1 fan. That seat's taken. However, feel free to take notes because the #2 slot is wide open and I'm accepting applications. You better be ready to work hard, soldier.

Humbly your favorite,
Phelba

FIRSTS

Joining the entertainment industry comes with its fair share of "firsts." I could pretend I floated into the music scene flawlessly, and you might believe me. But if I'm being honest, I felt more like I was wearing sweats to the prom. In preparation for my first tour, my manager got me several press opportunities, the first of which was on Marie Osmond's talk show.

The most surprising aspect of the experience was that Marie and I didn't meet each other until I sat next to her on the stage. We were given approximately ten seconds to say hello before the cameras started rolling, and then we had to act like we were already good friends. This was easy to do, since Marie is one of my idols, but after the cameras stopped she thanked me for being on the show and promptly vanished. It was a whirlwind. *So I guess this means we're not going out to lunch together?*

I've since learned that this is how it goes in showbiz. I had a similar experience when Amy Poehler interviewed me for her web series, *Smart Girls at the Party*. She was incredibly nice, we did our interview, and then—like Marie—she disappeared, leaving me to eat my lunch alone. In addition to not eating together, I was also disappointed that she wasn't hilarious on the set. I guess I expected her to have everyone in stitches the whole time, but that would be like her expecting me to answer every question with a violin melody. There is no doubt about it that Amy Poehler is one of the smartest and funniest girls at any party, but like every other human on the planet, she has a complete range of emotions and lives her own version of a normal life.

Just when I thought I was starting to get the hang of doing morning shows and guest performances, I was introduced to a whole new experience with European television. The first time I appeared on a German morning show I was given an earpiece with a real-time translator. As the interviewer spoke in German, I had to feign interest while trying to catch what my translator was saying in my ear. After every question there was a five- to ten-second delay while my translator finished the question in my ear, and I just sat and listened, and smiled, and felt stupid. It was a little awkward, but I can think of worse things. On that same trip, I also did a late-night show where the host acted as the translator. He talked to me in English and then turned to the crowd and spoke in German. Several times during this process the crowd burst into laughter, and I remember thinking, *What I said wasn't funny*. I deduced that he was either making fun of me, or making me seem more fun. I still don't know what he said, and part of me doesn't want to. I felt very uncomfortable, but again, I can think of worse things—like the time I accidentally told Josh Groban I had bad gas. Moving on.

One of my most anticipated performances was on *Conan*. When the stage managers came to give us our fifteen-minute call, I got out my violin to do a small warm-up and realized the tension in my bow was shot. I twisted the end and instead of getting tighter as it should, it spun loosely in my hand. I was going to be on live TV in less than fifteen minutes and I didn't have a bow! My manager, Adina, immediately found a stagehand and asked whether there were any other violinists in the band or on the whole Warner Bros. lot from whom we could borrow a bow. The stagehand disappeared and returned several minutes later holding three bows he'd dug out of the prop closet. One was completely fake and one was missing nearly all the bow hair. This left me with no choice but to use the last—an uneven fiberglass bow. I held it in my hands and said hesitantly, "I think it's real." In the remaining three minutes before my performance, I rubbed as much rosin as I could on the dirty bow hair and played a few scales to warm up.

I looked around at my band and crew. "It sounds okay, right?"

"Better than it would without . . ." Adina replied.

When I finally watched the replay on TV that night, I was mortified by the scratchy sound of my violin. For the next few days I dodged all phone calls from my family until I was ready to face the performance. When I solemnly confided in my mom, she laughed.

"That's hysterical!"

I'm glad she thought so.

Dipping my toes into the industry also meant occasionally brushing shoulders with other performers. One of the first times this happened, I was performing on *Dancing with the Stars* on the same night as Michael Bublé. At my rehearsal the day before I joked with the producer that I wouldn't mind if she put me in the dressing room next to his. When she walked me backstage the next night she smiled and nodded as we passed the sign above Michael's dressing room, which *was* conveniently next to mine. Later that night, she came into my room and told me it would be a good time to take a stroll down the hall (wink!). I opened the door and there he was, mingling with some people a few feet away. When I finally got up the courage to go say hi, he was so charming I actually thought he was enjoying our conversation. Then I remembered I was talking to the king of charisma and that he could vomit onstage and make it look magical. Regardless of whether or not he was really interested in my life, he acted the part well, and for that I will always love him.

Not all my hobnobbing opportunities ended as well as my conversation with Michael. In fact, I've botched quite a few first impressions over the years. Since I had a hard time narrowing it down to just one, I decided to include a few of my favorite celebrity run-ins.

JESSIE J

I love Jessie J. In fact, I think she is one of the best live performers ever, like *ever* ever. Unfortunately, my encounter with her was an epic fail. I have seen Jessie perform twice now, and most recently I played on an Australian morning show right after her. Of course she killed it, and when her set was over, she walked offstage and cordially thanked all the stagehands for their hard work. As she approached Erich and me, I hoped she might say something about my music. Instead, she looked us in the eye and said, "Thank you for your help with the set." Because I was surprised, I nodded and said, "You're welcome." She passed and I walked onstage, avoiding eye contact with Erich.

ASHTON KUTCHER

Another impression I wish I could erase took place at a Google event in London. After using the restroom, I was waiting for the elevator when I noticed a small table of complimentary mints, gum, and floss picks in the hall. *Why not*, I thought, as I grabbed a pick and began flossing. I was almost finished when the pick got stuck between my teeth, and of course that was also the moment the elevator doors started to open. I frantically tried to loosen the pick, with no luck. When I looked up, Ashton Kutcher was exiting the elevator in front of me. He nodded with a closemouthed smile, and I just gaped back at him—partially because I was looking at Ashton Kutcher, and partially because a floss pick was preventing my mouth from fully closing.

RICK ASTLEY

I grew up listening to Rick's smash hit "Never Gonna Give You Up," so when I saw him on the red carpet I was determined to get a picture. Adina pulled out her phone, and I politely asked Rick for a photo. As soon as we were standing side by side, a swarm of

Adina and me in Tokyo for press.

photographers attacked, like ducks on a breadcrumb. They shoved and shouted, until Rick raised a hand and said, "That's enough," like the seasoned superstar that he is. He walked away, and the photographers cleared, leaving Adina standing alone. Her head hung in shame. "I didn't get it," she whimpered. A few minutes later I poked my head into Rick's dressing room and asked for another picture, because I was never gonna give that up.

Although I wish some of my first impressions had been a little less uncomfortable, I don't get starstruck very often. Seeing famous people is always neat, but I also know they are just people. Whenever I run into old acquaintances or family friends, I hear the same things.

"I saw you did a video with Josh Groban. Looks like you made it!"

Or, "I watched you on *Conan*. You finally made it!"

I appreciate the enthusiasm. These experiences are always exciting for me, but I'm just hustling like everyone else. I've never thought of any one moment as a sign that I "made it." That is, until the night I met Taylor Swift.

She was hosting an after-party for the Billboard Music Awards, and somehow I got an invitation. I expected it to be a huge event and was worried there might be a cap on the guest list, so after the ceremony I packed up my things and went straight to the party—on the roof of Caesars Palace. Brooke and Adina were with me, and when we arrived, the doorman checked our names off a list and then gently told us we were the first to arrive.

"Oh, is Taylor up there?" I asked.

"No. But you are welcome to go up and wait."

"How embarrassing," Brooke said under her breath.

I've never felt so uncool in my entire life. Everyone knows you're supposed to be fashionably late to a party, especially an after-party! I turned around, grabbed Brooke and Adina by the arms, and said to the doorman, "We'll be back later. Don't tell anyone we were here!" He laughed and said he wouldn't, but I think he lied—little weasel. I can picture it now. Taylor Swift arrives at her party and asks the doorman if anyone has come by yet. He looks at his list.

"Of course not, that would be humiliating. Wait a minute . . . Yes, a girl named Lindsey Stirling was here *an hour ago.* . . ."

Oh, great! When we returned later, we walked out onto a patio and not more than twenty feet away stood Taylor Swift, Tim McGraw, Faith Hill, and Ed Sheeran in conversation. We were making our way casually to a fire pit on the other side of the roof when Taylor stopped midsentence and yelled, "Lindsey! Get over here!"

Adina, Brooke, and I emitted a collective shock wave that nearly leveled Las Vegas. We all froze, looking around for a different Lindsey who might cut me off the moment I began to run toward Taylor Swift with outstretched arms. When no one else appeared, I concluded she must have been talking to me. I walked to where she stood and we talked for several minutes, about what, I couldn't tell you. As she walked away to greet another guest, I looked back at Brooke and Adina with wide eyes.

"You never told me you knew Taylor Swift!" Brooke chided me under her breath.

"I don't," I whispered back.

"Oh . . . she's still behind you. Be cool."

She paused until Taylor passed, and then said in a whisper, "Oh my gosh, Taylor Swift just yelled your name across a room of famous people. You've made it!" She was half joking, but a little serious.

I would now like to take a moment to thank the doorman for outing me and putting my name on Taylor's radar. I would also like to point out that being thoroughly uncool can sometimes turn around and make you feel very cool indeed.

For the record, I didn't think it was possible for Taylor to be any nicer than she appears to be on camera, but she is. I wish I could tell you the nice things she said, but my mind was busy racing. *I can't believe I'm talking to Taylor Swift. How does she know my name? I'm so confused. And wow she's tall.* I was starstruck.

On the flip side, I was not starstruck by Snoop Lion inviting me to smoke weed in his trailer at a YouTube gala. I told him I had to finish ironing my underwear. I think he totally bought it.

NO-MAN'S-LAND

I know my lifestyle isn't exactly average, but I still consider myself very much an everyman. I drive a used car, rent a small house with two other girls, and I fly coach unless someone else is paying. I live as normally as my lifestyle will allow, yet my line of work makes it difficult for most people to relate to me on a social level. I don't have a normal nine to five; work never starts or ends. It just goes.

I was at a social gathering when someone asked me what I did for a living. When I told her I was a performer, she responded, "Wow, your life is so exciting! So what is it like to be famous?"

It's moments like this that I realize how uncomfortable I am in the social scene. I know my day-to-day is very different from most, but I don't feel famous. I feel like me, doing my job.

Most people find my life incredibly amusing, which also makes dating difficult. More often than not, my dates turn into unofficial interviews, and the longer I talk about my life, the less I feel like a normal human and the more I feel like a novelty. Even if a date does go well, a follow-up date is difficult when I travel several months out of the year. During one work trip, a boy I'd been out with a few times sent me a text that read, "Have fun in Japan!" Unfortunately, by the time I got the message I was already in New Zealand. Most people I meet can't keep up, even if they want to. Relating to people with more stable lifestyles is difficult for me, too. I am frequently told I need to date people in the entertainment industry, who can understand me and keep up with my crazy schedule. Unfortunately, being a Mormon in the industry puts me on a whole new level of unrelatable.

Exhibit A: the social gatherings. I get invited out for drinks all the time. I don't drink, and although it doesn't bother me when other people do, going out for drinks and not drinking isn't all that fun. I don't mind doing it from time to time, but it's not my favorite go-to activity.

Exhibit B: the common ground. Apart from our shared line of work, most of the people I meet on the job don't have a lot in common with me. A while back, I did a recording session with a well-known writer who spent half our time together talking about topics beyond my comfort zone. Sometimes (but not always) the stereotypes are true—sex, drugs, and rock 'n' roll. I felt like an outsider in my own sphere. Most of the people who relate to my values can't relate to my lifestyle, and the people who relate to my lifestyle can't relate to my values. I'm in No-Man's-Land.

Even with the gaps in my social life, there are two places I feel completely comfortable. The first one is being on tour with my crew. They understand my lifestyle, because they experience it with me on a daily basis, but they also respect my standards and allow me the security of being myself. On the road, I have everything I need (family, friends, and work) on one or two buses, and I love it. When I'm back "home" in LA, I miss all my tour comforts, and I often feel out of place. When my work life slows down, I usually feel lonely and sometimes even a little lost, which leads me to my second comfort zone: my parents' house.

My parents still live in the same house we moved into when I was eight. My room is now violet instead of green, but it's still the same cozy sanctuary it's always been. When I have a gap in work, my impulse is to travel home to visit my family for a few days. My mom spoils me with her homemade refried beans, we stay up till 1:00 A.M. watching musicals, and I catch up on several months' worth of lost sleep. During my last break between tours, I had a few days in which work was slowing down and, as usual, I booked a flight home to Arizona. I was all packed and ready to leave when the voice of reason in my head told me I should stop running away. As much as I love my family, I was using my frequent trips home to avoid the task of creating a normal social life. Begrudgingly, I canceled my flight. It was time to build some relationships in Los Angeles.

Around this time a girl from my church casually invited me to a surprise party for another girl from church. Although I didn't know Invitation Girl or Birthday Girl, I decided to go to the party anyway. Invitation Girl told me it was going to be a *Peter Pan*–themed party

and that I could dress up if I wanted. I play dress up for a living—during my concerts, music videos, and photo shoots—yet I still get excited over the idea of going to a party in costume. I was also looking forward to attending a social event where alcohol wasn't the main attraction. Who needs beer when you have a bomb diggity pirate costume?! I had recently finished working on my "Master of Tides" music video (which was pirate themed, for those who haven't seen it), so naturally I opted to go all out. I wore the coat, the boots, the sash, and the enormous pirate hat. As the final touch, I made a hook out of some tinfoil and went as the captain himself.

When I arrived at the party I walked through the door and scanned the crowd; I was the only pirate in the whole place. I think I saw one girl wearing a Tinker Bell T-shirt. Other than that, it appeared I was the only attendee who got, much less accepted, the costume memo. This was disappointing, but not devastating. Unfortunately, as the night went on, Invitation Girl kept introducing me to everyone by saying I was famous. The night was uncomfortable in more ways than one.

A few weeks later, I went to an album release party for Meghan Trainor. In an effort to engage in conversation, I turned to the man on my right and mentioned how much I loved Meghan's music. He looked at me and asked, "Who's Meghan?" I stared back at him in awe before responding, "Meghan Trainor . . . the girl that was on the stage a few minutes ago. This is her album release party."

"Oh, I didn't know. My publicist told me I should come. I'm a male model, and I just got back from doing some work in Paris with Premium."

Let me guess, your publicist told you to say that, too, I thought as I excused myself.

Industry parties are a lot of networking, name-dropping, and self-promotion—not my favorite chitchat. I spent the rest of the evening turning away drinks and shaking hands with slightly sloppy attendees. Suddenly, I missed being the random girl in a pirate outfit at a sober birthday party. Once again, I was floating in No-Man's-Land.

Standing out on purpose is one thing, but doing so by default takes a lot of energy and confidence. I'm proud of the things that set me apart, and I know why they are good; but that doesn't mean it isn't difficult. Every now and then I wish I wasn't the only one-piece swimsuit at the pool, the only sleeved dress on the red carpet, the only sober performer in the room, or the only pirate at the party. Not because I don't see the value in these things, but because sometimes being different feels a lot like being alone, and being alone is exhausting.

A few days after the industry party, I got the following e-mail from Erich.

Hey there little lady,

*I wanted to take just a second of your already hectic life and address a few things that have been playing on my mind regarding these last few months on tour. I just want to say thank you, on several levels. Being able to work with you has been a breath of fresh air after breathing very stale, tired, and grumpy club/arena air for the last sixteen years (but I guess that also depends on how close we stand next to each other). In all seriousness though, I have thoroughly enjoyed **you**, as a person, an employer, and an artist. I have never felt so honored to be a part of something growing the way this is, and I am truly excited for the future. I can also say I have never written a thank-you note to any other act or group I have ever worked for.*

God has truly given you a gift and I am so happy to see that you keep Him in your life every day, on the bus, and even in the venue. He is very much in every step you take and people recognize that. They may not know what it is they are seeing or feeling, but He is there in you. I always find it funny how the big gnarly crew guys have a lighter step at the end of the night than they had upon our arrival, and they always have a newfound smile on their face when you are present. God works in and through you in such a great way. I really do love being a part of your team and I am willing to back you in whatever way you are willing to have me along.

Thank you, from the depths of my heart, for a truly great experience. And please, please stay pure and healthy in mind, body, and soul because you still got a long way to go. So, breathe deep and breathe often.

Love and Thanks,
Tour Dad

It's moments like these that remind me I'm not actually living in No-Man's-Land.

CONFESSIONS

I have a few confessions to make. Since this book is a safe zone, I thought now would be a good time to bring them up.

CONFESSION #1

As hard as it is to believe, I don't like it when people leave comments on my photos or videos about how tired or sick I look. I know these remarks are made out of concern for my well-being, but no woman likes to be told she looks haggard—and we all know that's what "sick and tired" really means. More often than not, I'm healthy, well-ish rested, and not wearing any makeup. So there's that.

CONFESSION #2

A pillow preference is a very personal thing. Like brand loyalty to Oreos or deodorant, some things are better left unchanged. My pillow of choice is firm, and I absolutely cannot stand down pillows. They always look so fluffy, but when I lay my head down, it goes right through the middle and hits the bed. They might as well be made out of Jell-O. Sometimes when my hotel room has down pillows, I call the front desk and say I'm allergic. . . . It's not a total lie; I'm allergic *in my heart*.

CONFESSION #3

This one is hard for me, and it's probably going to break a lot of hearts, but I don't like Nutella. I took a picture with a giant container once, because it was a novelty size. The influx of Nutella sent by fans afterward kept me quiet for a long time, but I feel like I need to come clean. Next time, I'll take a picture with a puppy. Preferably a small puppy that doesn't bark, is housebroken, and likes to cuddle. Luckily, my lighting tech, Andy, does love Nutella. He sends his sincere thanks.

CONFESSION #4

I love to hide and scare people. Unfortunately, the guys aren't as easy to sneak up on as my mom is, so I've recently resorted to screaming, "I'm naked!" when they enter a room. I know, it's a cheap shot.

CONFESSION #5

I do not abide by expiration dates. I have a lot of faith in modern preservatives. Instead of reading labels, I follow the "look, smell, and taste" method.

CONFESSION #6

My favorite word is *tortellini*. I do not have an explanation for this. Say it five times in a row and tell me you don't love it.

CONFESSION #7

My least favorite word is *fester*. So many people have a problem with the word *moist*. That's how I describe a delicious cupcake or brownie. Moist treats do not bother me. But festering ones? I think I've made my point.

CONFESSION #8

When I am tired, I get super honest. For example, I once told Erich I had a raging wart on my heel that was snagging all my socks. I must be getting tired, because I wasn't going to tell you that, either.

CONFESSION #9

I think about breakfast as I am going to sleep, and it's the reason I get out of bed every morning. Once, I slept through the continental breakfast hours at a hotel and I cried a little. Go ahead, I'm judging myself.

CONFESSION #10

Unevenly spread peanut butter gives me anxiety. *You couldn't take two extra seconds to get it into the corners? My two-year-old self could* *make a more appetizing sandwich than that! Here *takes knife*, just step aside.*

CONFESSION #11

My crew has named two of my belongings "Smelly Sweaty Stinky Thing" and "Sadness 1." I don't feel safe enough to tell you exactly what they are referring to. Okay, fine, I'll whisper it. Lean in. Get closer. I don't stink right now! (The performance belt that holds my sound pack, and my wardrobe case.)

CONFESSION #12

I have to give myself a pep talk before every Phelba video I make, because she makes me as uncomfortable as she makes everyone else. Phelba has to commit 110 percent, otherwise it's just me talking about myself in a weird voice.

CONFESSION #13

There are few things I find less attractive than a drunk man, which brings me to my last and final confession.

CONFESSION #14

This one was confessed *to* me. A drunk A-list celebrity heartthrob once told me he was "a bad little girl." He also told me he would like to reserve the right to wear women's underwear from time to time. Gosh, it feels good to get that off my chest.

EVERYONE STARTS OUT
IN KHAKIS

When I think of my first job, two things come to mind immediately: accidentally sabotaging my best friend's interview and Tyler from customer service. It was the summer before my senior year of high school, and out of boredom, Michelle and I walked into the SuperTarget and applied for the same job. We were both invited in for a group interview scheduled for later that afternoon, and rather than going home to change into more professional clothing or brush our teeth, we spent two hours trying on shoes and flipping through greeting cards. During the interview the manager asked, "What does customer service mean to you?" Michelle smiled nervously and said something about "serving the customer." She was a genius in school, but under pressure she crumbled like overcooked bacon. I knew I could either come up with an equally insipid answer or blow her out of the water. When it was my turn, I smiled and said something about "giving the best experience possible to any customer, so they leave happier than when they arrived." I got the job, and she didn't.

For the next year and six weeks, I went to work every day in a red shirt and khaki pants, a color combo that makes me gag to this day. At first I was excited, because I got a walkie-talkie and a badge inscribed with my name spelled correctly. I felt very official. I also had a crush on Tyler from customer service and had fantasies about him calling my name over the walkie-talkie to meet him at his counter. When I arrived, he would pull me in for a kiss and tell me how good I looked in my uniform. It was all extremely thrilling. That is, until I realized the only purpose of the walkie-talkie was for my team leader to order me around the sales floor without having to speak with me face-to-face.

When I finally got promoted to work a cash register, I was ecstatic—you would have thought Tyler finally came through on the walkie. While working at the register, I must have claimed it was my first day for at least a month. It's amazing how quickly someone's face can go from frustrated to sympathetic when you say you're new. Consequently, every time I made a mistake when ringing someone up, I told them it was my first day. I did it for so long I started to worry I would get a returning customer, so I changed the wording a little. "This is the first time I've done this type of transaction, sorry."

"Oh, no problem, dear, take your time."

Working the register wasn't nearly as fun as I had hoped, but at least I could now buy an entire tank of gas at once. That's when I learned: Earning a paycheck is one of the best feelings in the world and wearing khaki capris is one of the worst.

You would think after the Target incident Michelle and I would have learned not to interview for the same job. But our freshman year in college we both applied for and miraculously got hired by a marketing company that sold health and energy gels. I guess it wasn't so miraculous considering Michelle's uncle was the owner, but I felt lucky nonetheless.

Our job consisted of making welcome calls to new health club customers and answering phone calls from unsatisfied ones. It was a small office. Besides Michelle and me, there were only three other employees: Brenda, who literally never stopped talking; Creepy

Carl, who popped up over the top of my cubicle every five minutes to ask unnecessary questions; and Craig, who always seemed high. We resorted to talking to loud and obnoxious Brenda to avoid the other two, who both got raises before we did. After a year of talking people into buying gels they would never use, Michelle and I both realized this was not our future. That's when I learned: If loud Brenda, Creepy Carl, and high-as-a-kite Craig could hold jobs, I could do anything.

I held a few other jobs here and there during college, but my last real gig before I ran off with my violin for good was as a counselor at a live-in treatment center for teenage girls. Unlike most correctional facilities, New Haven was an actual house with a kitchen, living room, big backyard, cherry trees, and a horse stable. There were no spiked gates, concrete walls, or barred windows. The lack of daunting restrictions made it feel like a home, but this also required us to wrestle a girl or two who made a break for the highway. The technical term for this is "placing a hold," which is code for "tackle and hang on." In spite of the occasional escape attempts, I enjoyed working at New Haven, because I felt like I was doing something beyond just making money. At first, I was worried about finding the correct balance between being cool and being effective. More than once, I was the recipient of an angry rant about how I was "the worst counselor ever!" At first, these outbursts hurt, but when all was said and done, the girls always preferred the tough-love counselors over the easygoing ones. They didn't want more freedom, they wanted to feel protected, grounded, and loved. Being able to provide that stability was one of the most rewarding feelings in the world. That's when I learned: I wanted a job where I could make a difference, but preferably without being screamed at.

As a performer, my life is everything I imagined and more. I live inside my imagination and get to see my ideas brought to life on a daily basis. I work in the environment I want, with the coworkers I want, at the pace I want. When all is said and done, I get a huge emotional payoff from the people who support and appreciate my music. Most important, I have the capability to make people feel significant and special, which is a humbling responsibility. But even in these ideal circumstances, I occasionally get tired and cranky and think about how nice it would be to have a normal workweek with weekends and vacation days again. It's times like these that I've learned: Even dream jobs feel like work some days.

If you don't have your dream job, keep working at it until you do. When you get there, don't forget it's your dream. Remind yourself what it felt like to wear khakis every day, and everything else will seem great in comparison. And if you're the one wearing the khakis, don't worry, it's not permanent . . . unless you want it to be. In that case, those capris look dang good on you.

ARTISTIC
MONSTER

When I was in film school I learned how to adjust lighting and edit a movie, but no one ever taught me how to pitch an idea to a board of directors or approach the industry without embarrassing myself. I think there must be an unspoken rule in any art-related community that to speak of mainstream success is a betrayal of the indie nature of art.

"Don't make art because you want it to be seen, do it because you love it," they say.

That's all fine, but everyone wants their art to be seen or heard. Isn't that why we make it?

At VidCon one year, I sat on a panel with a few other You-Tubers. Someone in the crowd asked me how I measure the success of my videos. I explained that first I have to be proud of the music I've created. But ultimately, if the music reaches and inspires my fans, then I've done my job. Another performer on the panel said the opposite—that he didn't need approval from his fans and that everything he did was in response to his own artistic values.

I have never compromised my tastes to fit into a mold, but of course I want my music to reach my fans and hopefully inspire them. I'll admit, when I release a project that isn't well received, it loses a bit of the magic. I'm not an automaton! Nothing is more thrilling than having fans understand my vision, and nothing is more disappointing than when they reject it. But alas, it's the name of the game, and I'm grateful I get to play it. So if anyone is wondering, I make art for the sake of art . . . *and for my own selfish gratification*, because I'm an artistic monster.

Speaking of being an artistic monster, when I first started my YouTube channel, I did everything besides the actual filming myself. I wrote and recorded the music, found the film locations, made my own costumes, did my own makeup, choreographed my dances, directed each scene, edited the video, and promoted it however I could. At first, I operated this way out of necessity. I cut costs wherever possible to scrape by. But as my music career progressed, I continued to function as a one-woman army by choice. I liked having my hand in every step of the process, and I felt comfortable knowing everything was getting done exactly the way I wanted it. Granted, there were times when it was normal for me to get an average of four hours' sleep every night, but at least I knew everything was happening on cue. I guess "artistic monster" is another term for *controlling*. *Controlling* sounds so negative. Let's use the term go-getter.

For years I worked under these circumstances, until Adina finally stepped in and forced me to delegate. I could afford to hire a few extra hands, but I couldn't afford to lose any more sleep. My "Stars Align" music video was one of the biggest productions I had ever done, and with some coaxing from Adina, I agreed to hire a director, producer, choreographer, and makeup artist. I remember the first day on set, watching everyone bustle around and feeling so replaced by my own crew. *What am I supposed to do?* I thought. I've since discovered a better balance between being involved and being overwhelmed. If I'm not sewing a cape at midnight, I can spend my time doing the things no one else can do for me.

Me, sewing a cape at midnight for the
Skyrim video I did with Peter Hollens.

Even though I have gotten better at delegating, there are still a few things I will always prefer to do myself. Number one on this list is editing. Sometimes I let other people take a first pass, but I usually insist on making the final cuts. I like to call it fine-tuning.

One time I did a video to promote a speaker company. When I saw their final edit, I noticed a few problems. I asked permission to make some changes, and they politely declined. When I asked them to reconsider, they said I could come into their office and sit with their editor as long as I wanted and suggest changes for him to make. When I do collaborations now, it is in my initial contracts that I get the final edit if need be. I'm really not as controlling as it sounds! Let me explain.

First of all, most editors don't play the violin. I can't tell you how many times I have received a first edit for one of my videos, only to find that half the violin shots are out of synch with the music. Even if they are able to match up the speed of my playing on video to the speed of the recording, the notes are often incorrect. A long note on the E string is not equal to a long note on the D string. Many people might not notice these details, but they are important to me as a musician. Second, most editors aren't dancers. As a result, they frequently choose a better camera shot over a sharper dance move. Also, most editors naturally like to cut on the beat. As a dancer, I would rather see a movement finish and cut a second later. And lastly, I've found that some editors unknowingly waste the magic.

I believe every good video contains a little magic between camera and performer. Sometimes I see a clip where my focus is elsewhere:

Don't trip on my dress.

Oops, I missed a note.

What is my next dance move?

In these moments, I might be moving correctly and playing all the right notes, but I am not connecting with the camera. When editors use one of these clips over another, it feels wasteful. I want to fill every moment with a little magic. As the creator and performer of my own music, I know every beat and every note more intimately than anyone else. I know what the music is calling for. I want to do the final edits. And I love doing it!

Other things I prefer to do myself include the initial storyboarding for music videos and tour content, costume design, and staging. I realize this makes me a bit of a diva when it comes to the way I like things done creatively. As a result, I often remind myself that just because someone does something differently doesn't make it wrong . . . but I'm still going to change it. I can't help it; I'm a monster! When I have costumes made, I usually make some adjustments of my own. If I don't feel like myself after I get my makeup done, I'll make a few final touches. And the directors I work with know by now I'll be giving suggestions throughout the whole shoot. Luckily I've found wonderful people to work with who can appreciate my involvement and don't see it as an insult to their own work.

I currently get an average of six hours' sleep every night, and it feels good. I also get fewer comments on my Instagram pictures about the bags under my eyes, so I appreciate that, too.

A STYLIST'S LIFE
FOR ME

At first, working with a stylist was a nightmare. I dislike shopping. I'd much rather spend my time making money than spending it. I'm also incredibly indecisive when it comes to clothing, and I have horrible buyer's remorse. That's why I always imagined having someone else pick out my clothes would rock. It did not.

For the first few years of my career, working with a stylist wasn't financially an option. I did all the costuming myself with very elementary sewing skills. (I know this comes as a shock after seeing my kangaroo costume, but my skill level plateaued shortly after that.) When I started doing projects that required more intricate outfits (for video game or character-based videos), I found a local seamstress who was willing to make my costumes for free, so long as she could sell them on Etsy when I was finished. When I moved to LA I had to leave this arrangement behind, but I continued to design and piece together my own costumes as best I could. On my first tour, I could only afford to have a few costume pieces made professionally. The others were Lindsey Stirling originals, patched together entirely from fabric and safety pins. As my music grew in popularity, however, so did the number of press opportunities and industry events I was expected to attend. And I was expected to wear something different to each one; I couldn't wear the same outfit on the *Today* show and *Conan*. From a publicity standpoint, each show wanted their own look and an exclusive photo for press releases. Expanding my wardrobe was more of a business decision than a personal one, but I felt like I was spending more time run- ning around the mall than I was working on my craft. I like looking nice as much as the next girl, but I have never worried much about my clothes. When all the kids in high school were wearing Aber- crombie & Fitch, I was sporting a baseball tee from the JCPenney clearance rack. (I originally spelled it *Amber*crombie . . . see what I mean?) As a developing musician, the last thing I wanted to do was go shopping a few times a week in search of something appropriate to wear at an interview. Half the time, I didn't even know what the appropriate attire should be! On top of press opportunities, I was constantly trying to design fresh new looks for music videos and live shows. A few days before my "Stars Align" video shoot I called my mom in a panic. It was my biggest production yet, and I still hadn't figured out what my eight dancers and I were going to wear.

"How can I create nine cool, affordable, danceable, tribal-like costumes that are modest in three days?" I asked her.

A loincloth and an animal print bikini top would have been such an easy fix if modesty weren't an issue. I lost two nights' sleep ago- nizing over it, and when I found a solution I spent another sleepless night making all nine costumes. This was frustrating. Losing sleep over an amazing idea or new song was one thing, but losing sleep over clothes? What a waste.

This went on for some time, before I decided to seek semiprofessional help. I wasn't ready to commit to hiring a real stylist yet, so I contacted a fashion blogger I liked and asked if she would be interested in helping me find some new clothes for an upcoming photo shoot. We met up in New York the day before my shoot, and she took me shopping at several high-end secondhand stores—where people recycled their grandmother's belongings and called them "vintage." Marina was living in New York City, and I invited her to come along. Every time I tried something on, the stylist would rain compliments on me like the best of them.

"Oh, that looks so cute on you! I love it! So classic grunge."

Marina, on the other hand, stood a few feet behind her shaking her head with a grimace. "Don't listen," she mouthed. I had to agree with Marina—I hated everything I tried on. In an attempt to be cooperative, I found a simple T-shirt I felt comfortable wearing.

"This one looks okay. Should I get it?" I asked.

Marina stuck her index finger through a gaping hole in the sleeve. "But it's eighty dollars . . ."

Point taken. I eventually bought a few things so the stylist wouldn't feel like I wasted her time, but on the subway ride back to Marina's apartment, I lamented. "I still don't feel like I have anything I can wear tomorrow!"

"We'll fix this," she said confidently.

Back at her place, we rummaged through my bags and her closet until we put together several cute outfits. I should have hired her instead.

My first experience working with a real stylist was also a bit of a fashion disaster. I imagine she thought the same thing about working with me. I'm a challenge for most stylists. My clothes must be modest in very specific ways. This means necklines can't be too wide or low, sleeves and skirts must be the correct length, and no see-through material without a slip. If I am performing, it also needs to be something unique, easy to move in, nothing too hot, and complementary to my performance dance sneakers. If a skirt is too short, I can't wear it; but if it is too long, I will trip. More than a stylist, I needed a genie. On top of these stipulations, most stylists prefer to work with designers, and finding a designer ensemble that adheres to my checklist is a real chore.

When my first stylist arrived, my heart dropped as I browsed gorgeous piece after piece that I knew I couldn't wear. The next time I did a styled event, she returned with a small selection of modest dresses. Most were hideous. The few that were cute were all just a few inches shy of appropriate in one way or another. This happens all the time. Some dresses are so close! But when renting from a designer, only minor alterations are allowed. What's that sound you're hearing? It's me, playing the world's smallest violin for myself.

Sometimes a stylist will bring a selection of clothes I can borrow, and other times I have to purchase them. Before my appearance on *Good Morning America*, the stylist pulled a selection of high-end clothes, none of which were for rent. Everything she brought was incredibly expensive and I kept looking at my options, thinking, *But I could find something similar at Forever 21 for a fraction of the price.*

"But this is designer," she said.

"Oh, right."

I felt like I was indulging in a child's game. I looked at her and thought, *She just doesn't get it,* and she looked at me and thought, *She just doesn't get it.* I ended up buying a pink skirt that made me look like a cupcake, because it was the cheapest item she had.

After this experience, I gave up. Heck, I'd been dressing myself for over two decades. Then one day Adina showed up with a new stylist who wanted to try working with me. Jessica Margolis, what an angel. I was getting ready for the *Today* show, and she asked me, "Do you want to look cute, or wear designer names?"

"Is Forever 21 a designer name?" I asked jokingly.

The next day she brought a rack of clothes from American Apparel, Forever 21, and Topshop. Everything was affordable, and I felt like myself when we were done. That's not to say I don't ever wear designer clothing. I do, sometimes. But it's not my top priority. Speaking of which, I wore a designer gown to the 2015 VMAs and earned a spread in the worst dressed list with Perez Hilton. I was offended, but a moment later I realized Perez Hilton thought *I* was worth talking about. He doesn't put just anybody on the worst dressed list. Ugly frocks are a dime a dozen, but he chose to mention mine! It was strangely flattering. By the way, the last time I saw Perez he was wearing spandex cloud-print leggings and a denim vest. Out of mutual respect I put him on my own mental worst dressed list. Don't worry, Perez, I got your back.

I might not have much interest in high fashion, but I adore costuming. If costume design were a man, I would marry him. Having someone to help me bring my ideas to life is like living inside a Cadbury egg—a dream come true. My costume design process starts with me sending Jessica ideas in the form of sketches or random pictures I find on the Internet. From there, she collects different clothes and has a few mock outfits pieced together, and we play dress up. She knows I like flowing skirts, bustled skirts, nonrestrictive sleeves, and MORE SEQUINS! Most important, she gets me, helps me stay modest, makes me feel beautiful, and keeps me from worrying about my wardrobe so I can focus on the things that really matter— like Phelba's wardrobe for *her* next video. Speaking of which, has anyone seen my gaucho pants?

POST-TOUR
BLUES

Erich knows my schedule better than I do, and every night on tour he sends out a day sheet so we all know what our tomorrow holds. Here's a pretty typical day in Chicago, Illinois.

LINDSEY STIRLING UNTIED STATES OF AMERICA

FRIDAY, JUNE 5TH   **CHICAGO, ILLINOIS**

SHOW DAY   **CHICAGO THEATRE**

VENUE   **MIKE/DRIVER HOTEL**

Chicago Theatre   **JW Marriott**
175 North State Street   151 West Adams Street
Chicago, IL   Chicago, Illinois

TODAY:

8:30 AM	WALK THROUGH/BREAKFAST
9:30 AM	LOAD IN
12:00 PM	LUNCH
12:15 PM	DEPART FOR RADIO, One Prudential Plaza, 130 E Randolph Street. ste 2700. Mary Ellen
3:30 - 5:00	LINDSEY SOUND CHECK
5:00 - 6:00	KARMIN SOUND CHECK
6:00 - 6:45	CAILEE RAE SOUND CHECK
5:30 PM	DINNER
5:30 - 6:30	MEET AND GREET
6:30 PM	DOORS
7:30 - 7:50	CAILEE RAE
8:00 - 8:45	KARMIN
9:00 - 10:30	LINDSEY STIRLING
2:00 AM	BUS CALL

TONIGHT TRAVEL

Bus will travel 301mi 4hrs 37min to
Bunbury Music Festival at Sawyer Point Park 705 east Pete Rose Way Cincinnati, OH

TOMORROW   **SATURDAY JUNE 6TH**   **FESTIVAL DAY**

10:00 AM LOAD IN
5:30 - 6:30 SHOW TIME

A tour is one giant breathing organism, made up of different people and jobs—each equally necessary to keep the beast alive. Since everyone involved works so closely for the same end goal, there is usually a collective tour emotion at any given moment.

THE BEGINNING OF TOUR—EXCITEMENT!

In the beginning there is always a general feeling of excitement. We've all made it through several grueling rehearsals, and things are finally starting to come together. The days leading up to the first performances are usually filled with technical difficulties and exhaustion, but ready or not, here we come! Troubleshooting is inevitable, but seeing the show finally come to life is exhilarating. Even if my in-ear monitors cut out and Gavi's keyboard stands fall over during opening night.

THE MIDDLE OF TOUR—COMFORTABLE

Days feel longer on tour, and two weeks might as well be two months when you're around the same people 24/7. By the middle of tour, everyone has found their routine and things get very comfortable, maybe a little too comfortable. This is the point when all the guys fart themselves into early-morning existence without apology. This is also the time when my body starts to ache and my muscles turn to Jell-O.

THE END OF TOUR—EXHAUSTION

This is when talk of bowel movements becomes acceptable. Don't tell me about your food poisoning or how you slept in the bathtub until the last week of tour, because at that point, I've probably got food poisoning, too, and will want to tell someone about it. The excitement and adrenaline we get from performing never changes, but we all slow down a little between shows. My crew is especially tired at this point. They are the first ones up and unloading the equipment into the venue every morning, and the last ones loading the trucks at the end of the night.

At the beginning of tour, days off are mini-vacations when we all go sightseeing and spend time together. At the end of tour, days off are literally days spent *off* our feet. Once, with the exception of using the bathroom and answering the door for room service, I didn't leave my bed for an entire day. My body was tired, my brain was tired, and I didn't have any clean clothes to wear even if I wanted to go out. That's what the end of tour looks like.

LAST WEEK OF TOUR—NOSTALGIA

During the last week I get my second wind and I start to miss everything about tour before it's even over. I don't want it to end! I always treat my team to an end-of-tour dinner, where we reminisce about our favorite moments and I get sentimental (cue Vitamin C's "Graduation" song).

AFTER TOUR—END-OF-TOUR BLUES

No matter how tired I may be at the end of tour, I always get a bad case of the end-of-tour blues. I think most people who've lived on the road can relate to the low of coming off.

This transition has gotten a little easier over the last few years, but I always hate waking up the next day in my own surroundings. It's home, but I always feel so displaced. Living without constant human interaction is weird. Sleeping on a stationary bed is weird. Eating alone is weird. Not having a day sheet telling me what to do and where to be is weird. One minute I'm performing for several thousand screaming fans, and the next I'm in the frozen foods section of the local mini-mart and nobody cares. My body also goes through adrenaline withdrawal, which causes a temporary, chemical-imbalance-induced depression. This adrenaline downer happens to a small degree after individual shows sometimes, so you can imagine how much worse it is when I stop performing cold turkey. By the end of tour, my body has gotten used to a chemical schedule. I perform and get an adrenaline rush, it goes through my system, and the next night I do it again. Then suddenly I'm not doing anything but sitting in meetings or interviews, and my body is like, "What the heck, man, where's all my adrenaline? This is boring, I'm so depressed." And I have to be like, "Chill out, body, it's not the end of the world. You'll get more adrenaline when it's time!" The first time the sadness hit I didn't understand why it was happening, but after spending six to nine weeks on a natural high, my body has to come down one way or another.

Along with the physical adjustments, my mind usually encounters a small identity crisis as well. On tour, I have one clear purpose. When I get home I work just as much, but it's not as focused. Most people know the job they will be doing next week, next month, next year. I know I will still be Lindsey Stirling the musician, but I can't tell you what my days will look like until I get to them. Some days it's my job to write music, record, plan music videos, or meet with producers and directors. Other days it's my job to perform at one-off concerts and private events, do phone interviews, in-person interviews, written interviews, answer e-mails, edit videos, keep up with social media, plan my next tour, and right now I'm working on this book (*zing!*). But what am I *really* doing? And why? Where am I going to be in two weeks, or two years? What's my end goal? And tell me, what's my purpose today? Stepping onstage and making several thousand people happy is a lot easier and less complicated than all of *that*.

Even though touring/traveling takes up the majority of my time (seven to eight months of the year), I have to remind myself that tour life isn't real life. It's a world in which everything revolves around me, and as wonderful as that is, it's far from normal. On the road, it is Erich's job to make sure I'm happy and healthy, and he's really good at it. The food I like appears as if by magic, my clothes come back washed and ironed, my days are organized and coordinated for me, I see my name plastered on billboards and marquees, and I'm surrounded by people who love, support, and entertain me endlessly. Going home is hard because I forget what real life feels like. Who are my friends? Where do I hang out on weekends? What do I know how to cook? After coming off tour, I went to the grocery store and couldn't remember what meals I liked. I ended up calling my mom and asking her, "What do people make for dinner?"

The end-of-tour blues are inescapable, but I've picked up a few tactics to help me adjust more quickly. First of all, I always have a full schedule waiting for me when I get home. Some people would tell me I should take a break and relax, but there is nothing worse than going from a whirlwind into a vacuum. I also meditate twice a day every day. It makes me feel more in control of my mind and body, even when my emotions are trying to go AWOL. And I eat acai bowls, lots of acai bowls. In the end, I always remember who I am, and my home life starts to feel comfortable again, just as I am packing for my next trip. My life is a pendulum, always swinging back and forth. But the back is just as good as the forth. Sometimes I need a little time to remind myself of that.

STICKS AND
STONES

You can spend your whole life feeling small
by looking up at everyone above you, or you
can look down and see how far you've come.

"Sticks and stones may break my bones, but words will never hurt me." What genius came up with that one? A robot? What a load. Let me set the record straight. Throwing sticks and stones is mean (and archaic), but if you really want to hurt me, use words. They are much more effective.

When I was a senior in high school, I took private music lessons from a man named Arthur Dumont. At my first lesson he looked over the top of his spectacles and said, "From now on, everything you play reflects me. I don't like being embarrassed."

When he spoke, his fluffy white mustache bounced up and down like spiccato. There was no denying he was an incredible musician, but he was also the worst violin teacher I ever had. It's impossible to be effective when ego takes precedence over education. I was a replaceable pawn, a demonstration of his accomplishments.

For a while, I was determined to impress him and I did exactly what he said. My hand position improved, my straight-laced pinky relaxed, and my intonation was nearly perfect. He dictated my every move, and I listened. Until I realized I had lost the freedom to express myself, which was what had made playing music enjoyable in the first place. Like the computerized backtrack to a karaoke song, I was always on cue, but devoid of feeling. Practicing became a chore. Then one day I showed up to my lesson unprepared. Midterms were coming up, soccer playoffs were in full swing, and I was trying to finish up my college applications before the holidays. Needless to say, I hadn't touched my violin all week. I faked my way through the warm-up, but halfway into my concerto he held up a hand in disgust.

"Stop, stop, stop. Did you practice this week?"

I lowered my violin before answering. "I've had a lot going on—"

"Did you practice, yes or no?"

". . . No."

Immediately he knocked the sheet music from my stand, sending pages in every direction. Then, pointing to the door, he said barely above a whisper, "You have wasted enough of my time. Get in your little white car, and don't *ever* come back." He walked out of the room, leaving me to gather my sheet music off the floor.

When I told my mom what had happened I downplayed it. Good riddance, right? But it hurt a lot more than I wanted to admit, and it planted an insecurity I didn't notice for years. That was the last private lesson I took for nearly a decade.

Obviously, this did not destroy me. I later found my place in music—writing and performing songs I love and am proud of, songs that make me feel alive every time I step onstage. Then, when I was twenty-eight, I was invited to play with the famous singer Andrea Bocelli and the iconic Royal Philharmonic Orchestra. I may not be an active player in the classical community, but I am no stranger to it. I played in classical orchestral groups for twelve years before going rogue. Performing with Bocelli and the Royal Philharmonic was a huge honor. I accepted it with gusto and was sure it would be the experience of a lifetime.

Within minutes of arriving at my first rehearsal, all the excitement drained from my body, instantly replaced by insecurity and fear. From the moment I opened the door the resentment in the room was palpable. Bocelli didn't say a word to me the entire day, and the musicians in the orchestra used his open disapproval as an invitation to follow suit. I hadn't played a classical solo or followed a director in years, and there I was making a comeback in front of a few hundred professional musicians at The O$_2$ arena in London. What was I thinking? When I made mistakes, they giggled, and when I missed my entrance, they rolled their eyes. I had been promised ample rehearsal time so I could get comfortable with the music, but after one run-through of the songs, everyone got up to leave. For a professional classical musician, this would have been enough, but I hadn't been in this situation in years. The next day we did one more final run-through. When we were finished, Bocelli cocked his head to the side and said, "Better." It was the only word he said to me the entire time. I heard a few of the violinists chuckle under their breath.

When I finished my first performance on opening night, I didn't get a single gesture of recognition from either Bocelli or the conductor. Before the applause from the audience had even died down the orchestra went into the next song. It was as if I didn't exist. I've dealt with hate mail and hurtful comments since my introduction to YouTube, but I have never before felt hated like I did in that moment.

A little nervous energy onstage is invigorating, but fear is crippling. As the night went on, I second-guessed everything I played and felt disgust from the orchestra reflected tenfold. When I came back onstage for the final bow at the end of the night, Bocelli and another soloist grabbed hands and bowed with their backs to me. His disappointment couldn't have been clearer if he had booed into the microphone.

The next night, as I prepared to go out to the slaughter once more, the stage manager stopped me.

"Oh, you don't need to go on yet. Bocelli cut your first song from the concert."

I stood there, clutching my violin to my chest. He cut my solo because I wasn't good enough, an embarrassment even, and he didn't have the decency to tell me before the show. Seconds later, the music started and I realized they hadn't actually cut the song. They were just playing it without me. The first chair violinist took my part and played it flawlessly. A few songs later I had to go onstage and stand in front of the disapproving orchestra again. When I finished playing, I looked in their eyes and saw Arthur Dumont saying, "You have wasted enough of our time. Get in your little white car, and don't ever come back."

I forced a smile for the crowd and made it backstage before the sobs hit. I stayed for one more performance, but after another humiliating night of scoffs and downcast gazes, I packed up my things and left. It was really embarrassing and awful, and I cried. But worse than the way they treated me was the way I treated myself afterward. This experience taught me a few things about myself.

1. I care what other people think about me.
I've always thought I had pretty thick skin, but the looks of disgust I got from those professional musicians made me doubt everything I was doing. For years I've gotten hurtful comments from anonymous people trying to bring me down, but it wasn't until this experience that I considered what they were saying might actually be true. For the next several months I read comments on the Internet and took them to heart. I deserved it. They were right. I wasn't that good.

2. I was an even bigger bully than Bocelli and the Royal Philharmonic combined.
Bocelli and the Royal Philharmonic wanted to make sure I knew they were better than me, I have no doubt about that. It worked, obviously. Afterward, I wanted to blame them for crushing my confidence and drowning me in fear. But that was my choice. Ultimately, the responsibility fell on me. They may have knocked me down, but I was the one holding myself there. I let these feelings of doubt

and insecurity overcome me, until my inadequacies completely overshadowed my strengths. I lost sight of what I actually do, and I couldn't see the value in any of it.

3. I don't need to be the best.

When I got back from London I was in a dark place. On top of feeling inadequate, I was also overcome with guilt. I had been playing sold-out shows all over the world, when there were clearly other violinists more talented than me, who deserved success more than I did. Of course, I already knew I wasn't the best violinist in the world (or even close), but for some reason this experience opened up an insecurity I didn't know existed. Not long after, I came across some positive comments on the Internet, and I was reminded why I do what I do: to bring people joy. Am I the best violinist in the world? No. Do I need to be the best to bring people joy? No.

I know there are other violinists out there who can play with clearer tone, vibrato, and intonation than I can. They can play Mendelssohn, Tchaikovsky, and Bartók with better technique and accuracy. I applaud their talent. But I too have talents. I have my own strengths, which are not directly comparable to those of the Royal Philharmonic or Bocelli, and I'm trying to be okay with that.

In 2014, my name appeared in the *New York Times*. With genuine excitement, a friend e-mailed me the link to the article before reading it himself. I was ecstatic, until I started reading and realized the review wasn't a favorable one. In fact, it was a discourse between an EDM editor and a classical music editor, discussing how and why I had gained popularity making "competent but unoriginal dance music." Both made arguments as to why I fell short in either music category. Among other things, one of them said, "I kept trying to listen and the music would just fade into the background. So who's listening?"

Other reviewers have had similar reactions to my life's work.

"There's not nearly enough variance in Stirling's vaguely moody melodies, and her playing consistently favors frenzy over emotion."

"Its static nature and lack of development can only be described as banal. It is non-offensive music, played in a pretty way. . . . At least she holds her instrument beautifully . . ."

Not everyone is going to like what I do, the same way not everyone likes chocolate—which is baffling to me—but you don't see Mars bars running from the shelves in shame. (I have also never seen anyone speak condescendingly to a candy bar, but that is beside the point.) I don't claim to be the best musician. If being the best means I earn the right to look down on people and critique their accomplishments in defense of my own, I don't ever want to be. People can say what they want about my music being "banal" and my skill level "competent," and it will hurt my feelings (because despite what some believe, I do still have them), but I won't let it determine my self-worth. I still take lessons, I'm working on my skills, and I practice as often as I can. Maybe my best isn't as good as someone else's, but for a lot of people, my best is enough. Most important, for me, it's enough.

"AND WHAT ATTITUDE ARE YOU WEARING TODAY?"

I'll admit, before experiencing it firsthand, the words *red carpet* always inspired images of glamour and excitement. I don't want to spoil the allure, but there was a time when I would have preferred a gynecologist appointment to attending a red carpet event.

My first experience walking a red carpet was in Germany, circa 2012. I was performing at a charity event for breast cancer, and upon my arrival the event coordinator informed me I would be walking the carpet that evening. This was news to me, and I didn't have anything besides pajamas and a performance outfit in my small suitcase. When I shared this with her she replied, "It does not matter, you are the artist." Good to know. I didn't even bring heels, so I ended up wearing an old pair of Converse shoes and leg warmers with my outfit. This was before I had a publicist (or a manager, for that matter) so I had no one to plead my case to the press. Luckily, it was a small event and I was one of only a few performers that evening.

That night on the carpet a kind reporter stopped me and asked, "And who are you wearing tonight?" I remember feeling a strange sense of pride as I smiled back at her mischievously. I leaned in, as if I was telling her an earth-shattering secret, and confided, "I bought this dress on sale at Forever 21!" For some reason I thought she would be impressed to hear I had spent less than fifty dollars on my entire outfit. After all, she obviously couldn't tell the difference between my wardrobe and the next Dolce & Gabbana gown. Instead, she looked disappointed and moved along to the next, more appropriately dressed attendee. I watched her turn away and thought, *But I'm the artist?!*

After attending a few larger events, I learned arriving underdressed isn't the only way to be overlooked. On the carpet, everyone has a publicist who precedes them and makes introductions to different reporters. They walk around, spouting off information in a desperate attempt to get some airtime.

"This is Lindsey Stirling, an electric violinist whose latest album topped the *Billboard* charts at number two."

It's very uncomfortable, standing around in fancy clothes waiting for someone to take the bait and show some interest. Not to mention how unfortunate it is to be followed by someone more popular, which, at my level, happens a lot. No one wants to talk to

Lindsey Stirling if it means there is a chance they could miss out on interviewing Katy Perry. All the while, it's very important to act natural—even when reporters shove you aside midsentence to approach someone with more clout. Keep smiling, there are cameras everywhere! I should also mention that for every hour of the ceremony you see on television, there are several hours of sitting and waiting beforehand. This is the perfect time to compare yourself to others and recount all the reasons you should feel insecure.

When my second album came out I returned to the red carpet—for the Billboard Music Awards. I had a more suitable outfit on this time, but the experience was only slightly better because of it. By this point in my career I felt as though I had earned my place, but by the end of the night, the only thing I really earned were fresh blisters on my feet. I was presenting that evening, and I spent the whole day feeling shunned and unappreciated. I didn't get a dressing room, no one knew who I was, and security kept asking to see my pass when I was backstage. People were rude because I didn't have a familiar face, and on the red carpet there were lines of reporters trying to talk to the more prominent people ahead of and behind me. I felt like a horse on display (an unpopular one at that), being ponied down a line of press, trying to win everyone's bet. It was exhausting. I decided award ceremonies weren't really my thing.

A few months later I was invited to present and perform at the Country Music Television Awards. Though I felt flattered, I was immediately overwhelmed with dread. What if I didn't belong? From a business standpoint it was an incredible opportunity, so I went. I won't pretend I wasn't nervous.

When I arrived, I was put in a dressing room with several other people, one of whom was a popular country music artist who will remain nameless. She didn't speak to anyone, took up half the room with her personal things, and brought an entourage to respond to her every whim. Every time she left the room several people on walkie-talkies began speaking at once.

"She is on the way to hair and makeup, I repeat, she is on the way to hair and makeup. Over."

All the while, I sat on a sofa in the corner throwing the world's most extravagant pity party for one. I was about to start a thrilling game of solitaire when Jennifer Nettles sat down next to me and introduced herself, with the most endearing Southern twang. She said more encouraging and complimentary things to me in the next five minutes than I had said to anyone all day. It was incredibly humbling. After the ceremony, Florida Georgia Line approached me to compliment my performance, and Hunter Hayes went out of his way to congratulate me on my new album. I was pleasantly surprised by how much I enjoyed myself and I realized how selfish my approach to the evening had been. I had agreed to attend because I knew performing at the CMTs was a good opportunity to be seen and heard. That was all. I could just as easily have said hi to Jennifer Nettles, or complimented Florida Georgia Line, or congratulated Hunter Hayes. Instead, I waited for them to come to me because I was so worried and consumed with looking out for number one. I've since learned that the only way to really enjoy myself at these "glamorous" events is to forget about myself entirely. Sound familiar? I learn this lesson a lot, but every time I learn it a little quicker. Maybe someday I will learn it for good.

In 2015 I graced the red carpet once more, for the Billboard Music Awards. This time, *I* was determined to be the Jennifer Nettles of the event. Instead of feeling insecure and awkward, I spent my time between interviews reaching out to compliment the other people around me. I was still one of the less popular performers at the event, but I actually had a wonderful time. At one point I saw the girls of Fifth Harmony backstage, so I introduced myself and congratulated them on their new single. They smiled and nodded politely. A few minutes later I passed the real Fifth Harmony in the halls and I realized I had been talking to Pitbull's backup dancers about their "summer hit." Thanks, girls, for pretending to know what I was talking about. My attempt to "Jennifer Nettles" you might have fallen short, but I meant what I said about your hair being on point.

Me and not Fifth Harmony.

MY CAR

A few years ago I was invited to a Capitol Records party. It was a fancy affair, with a lot of industry bigwigs and cocktails. After the evening was over, Gavi and I were waiting at valet parking when we heard a car slowly rattling around the corner from the lot. Everyone within earshot turned to look. When Gavi saw it was my 2002 Toyota Echo making the earsplitting sound, his eyes got wide and his jaw hit the floor.

"No!" he mouthed in shock. "Linds, that's *your* car!" He buried his face in his hands. "You need a new car."

I get this all the time—people telling me I need a new car, as if I'm unaware of how "old" mine is. I'll admit, the rattling engine was a little embarrassing, but I got it fixed as soon as I had the time.

Admittedly, I could name a few other problems with my car. For starters, she's almost up to 200,000 miles, makes a screeching sound when I slow down, and gets a little jumpy in second gear; but who uses second gear anyway? The air-conditioning is also a little temperamental, but I discovered if I permanently removed the glove box I can reach my hand up underneath the dashboard to start the fan manually with my finger. Piece of cake. Most people see my car's quirks and think I should put it to rest. What they don't understand is, this car and I, we go way back.

When I was a teenager, the Echo was the "good car" in our family (meaning it was the one with air-conditioning), and driving it was a privilege. When I left for college, my parents handed me the keys and a map with the road home traced in yellow highlighter. I learned to drive a stick shift in this car, I practically lived out of it as a traveling musician, I drove it to LA to chase my dreams, and I currently spend several hours a week sitting in it on the 405. I think it's safe to say this car knows me better than most of my closest friends. You could say I'm a little sentimental about it, but ultimately, I haven't replaced the Echo because it still works.

"But you can afford it," some say.

I've never understood this mentality. Simply having the money to buy a new car means I should? I guess I should also buy a pontoon boat, or a camel, or a hot air balloon. Granted, a new set of wheels is much more practical than any of the above, but if it ain't broke, why fix it? My parents always drove used cars, and they didn't replace them until they had to be pushed off the road.

I remember when "the Babe" finally hit the dust. She was a gray 1990 Toyota Previa that saw me through my entire childhood and nearly ten family road trips to Rocky Point, Mexico. I was twelve when the air-conditioning broke, and I overheard my mom tell my dad it would cost $1,600 to get it fixed. At the time, it had over 150,000 miles, and they both assumed it wouldn't last long enough to justify the expense. Five years later, my mom was still driving it around Arizona like a giant rolling toaster oven. During the summer, she did most of her errands in the early mornings. When we had to get around during the day, we rested our necks on ice packs that melted quickly, leaving a mixture of water and sweat dripping down our backs. We also rode with the windows down and wore minimal clothing. On family vacations, my parents took out the middle seat and let us kids sit on the floor picnic style to distract us from the heat. It was a hot, exciting, and slightly hazardous system.

One summer my sisters and I needed vaccinations before going back to school, and the only available opening was in the middle of the day. When we finally arrived after the thirty-minute drive, the doctor took our temperatures and we all had fevers. My mom put her head in her hands and let out an exasperated laugh.

Despite the Babe's shortcomings, I loved driving her in high school. It was the only vehicle that could fit all my friends, making it the unanimous car of choice on the weekends. In addition to the broken AC, the dashboard lights didn't turn on, and the front passenger door was permanently locked. Accidental speeding at night was inevitable, and whoever rode shotgun had to climb in and out through the window; we were the cooler version of a clown car. Instead of letting it become an embarrassment, it became a symbol of our friendship. Then one day of my senior year in high school, on the way to Melody Smith's eighties-themed birthday party, the Babe rolled to a stop at the light on Pecos Road and never started up again. After that, my parents bought a white 1991 Chevy Suburban that Brooke and I named "Sub Zero." It lacked air-conditioning and a radio, but it pulled Brooke's horse trailer around town and had enough room for all my friends, so we didn't complain.

When I first moved to LA I spent a lot of time with my new management at the Atom Factory office. After I had been there for several months, one of the office assistants pulled me aside and asked, "So what's with the car?" Apparently everyone in the office had been buzzing about my sweet ride. They all wanted to know why I didn't drive something nicer.

At one point, Adina even tried to stage a car intervention. I went through a phase where I really wanted a smart car or a MINI Cooper, so she hooked me up with BMW, and they gave me a Cooper to drive for a week. It was candy-apple red with blue interior lighting, and we zipped around town like we were made for each other. At the end of the week, they offered me the car at a discount. My mouth started to water, but I passed. This was probably baffling to Adina—why didn't I want the car?! I guess it comes down to the fact that I don't have a lot of "normals" left in my life. But I do have my used car, which reminds me of the cars my parents always drove (and still drive) and the cars I grew up driving. When I'm in my Echo, it feels like a piece of home.

I want to be clear that I'm not preaching new-car abstinence. If you've earned it, go for it! I spend a lot of money elsewhere, on things I think are necessary to advance my career—music videos, studio time, touring—and sometimes I worry these things put me a little out of touch with reality. Luckily, I am still surrounded by friends and family who live humble and beautiful lives. Driving my trusty car makes me feel connected to them and to my upbringing. Someday I'm sure I'll buy a newer car with a better safety rating and automatic windows (I'd even take a cassette player). But probably not until I have to push my Echo off the road. This car and I, we go way back.

BEST
FOR LAST

Originally, I planned to end this book with a chapter about winning a Grammy for Best Contemporary Instrumental Album. It was going to be one of the best moments of my life! Unfortunately, I didn't make it past the early nomination phase. For those of you who aren't familiar with how the process works, anyone in the business can pre-nominate themselves for a Grammy. Following this, all initial nominees go before a committee, who ultimately vote on the final nominations. In my category, I felt confident I was the front-runner and everyone I knew was stroking my ego like it was a soft kitten. I had it in the bag. You can imagine my disappointment when I opened this hypothetical bag and there was nothing inside. Not even a consolation cookie.

For professional reasons, I had already told people in the industry I was going to be at the Grammys on February 8, 2015, and my management made plans around winning the aforementioned award. When I heard I was out of the running, I crawled away from the scene with my tail between my legs. "Actually, I am not going to be busy after all . . ."

In frustration, I called my mom. I complained that no one in the industry took me seriously, and said I was sick and tired of having to hustle just to prove I belonged. What did I have to do to earn a little respect in the music community? It's moments like these that I forget how far I've already come, and how lucky I am to be holding an empty Grammy nomination bag in the first place. It would have been really cool to be the first YouTuber to win one, but it would also be really cool to make music and travel the world for a living . . . ahem.

A few weeks after I *didn't* win a Grammy, Adina contacted me to let me know I had been chosen as part of Forbes's 30 Under 30 in Music for 2015. I dropped my empty Grammy bag like a hot potato so I could call my mom. I was pretty embarrassed at how upset I had been about being overlooked for the Grammy, and I was equally embarrassed when I realized it had taken a different prize to get me over it. Recognition is good for the soul, but my self-worth shouldn't have been dependent on the opinions of others. It's a lesson I've had to learn and relearn. In fact, these last few years I have been slipping and sliding up and down one giant learning curve. I've had to learn who to trust and how to delegate. I've learned to find value in my own integrity and when to say no to opportunity. I've learned how to share myself with the world and be comfortable with the criticism that may follow. I've had to learn how to dance on a hot stage for ninety minutes without passing out. And I've had to learn to live in the present, rather than in spite of it.

Once upon a time I thought I blew the greatest moment of my life. I no longer believe that is possible. Life is kind and full of great moments, but I think the greatest moment of my life is always ahead of me. When I reach it, there will be another, greater moment to come.

One of the questions I get asked the most in interviews is "Where do you see yourself in five or ten years?" More has happened in the last three years than I ever thought possible. I can't begin to imagine what the next five or ten years will hold. I don't even know what next year will bring! I spend a lot of time planning for what's next:

my next show, my next tour, my next album, my next music video. It's part of the job. But I want to spend more time balancing in the present. It's the only thing that truly exists. If I'm too busy ruminating over the past or pining for the future, some of those great moments will pass by before I get the chance to live in them. I don't want to look back and recognize some of my great moments in hindsight, after the opportunity to enjoy them has come and gone.

I put my favorite moments into the pages of this book, but I have to believe the best chapters are yet to come. I don't know what they are yet, because if I look too far into the future, I could miss out on what's happening right now. I imagine those chapters will involve my violin, the people that love and inspire me, and a lot more learning. Writing this book has been one of my great moments. Thank you for sharing it with me. Here's to the greatest moments of all our lives.

Fair Winds and Godspeed,
Lindsey

P.S.

It's Grammy nomination time again, and Adina just called to inform me that the most promising award I'm eligible for this year is Best Boxed or Special Limited Edition Packaging. . . . I have it in the bag!

FOR THE PEOPLE
WHO HAVE A SPECIAL
PLACE IN MY HEART, I MADE
A SPECIAL PLACE IN MY BOOK

Adina Friedman—Aside from my own mother, no one cares more about my well-being than this lady. Sometimes I email her at 3:07 A.M., and she replies around 3:08. She is my manager, my travel buddy, and the more organized half of my brain.

Ty Stiklorius—One of the most influential women in the music industry, and the reason I still believe it is possible to be a business powerhouse and a successful wife/mother.

Jani Dix—Our sophomore year of college she found me crying in the bathroom, trying to fix a terrible haircut I had given myself. She handed me a beanie and took me out for ice cream. Life has taken us in different directions, but I know I can always count on her for a hypothetical beanie and ice cream cone when I need it most.

Kaitlyn Tanner—On my mission I taught her how to walk fast and talk to strangers. She taught me how to love deeper and find the goodness in everyone. Being her companion was one of the greatest blessings of my mission. Being her friend since has been one of the greatest blessings of my life.

Aimee Patton—Living proof of the power of faith and perseverance. In my youth she was a loving mentor, and in my adult years she has become a dear and unwavering friend.

IN LOVING MEMORY OF
JASON GAVIATI
April 27, 1980–November 21, 2015

Gavi passed away after the completion of this book, but before it was published. Losing him was the darkest period of my life, but he will always be a light in my memory. When I think of him, I will always imagine him laughing, because that's what Gavi was best at—making people laugh and spreading joy. I love you, Gavi. I love you more than you will ever know.

ACKNOWLEDGMENTS

First and foremost, thank you to Mom and Dad Stirling, for teaching us that dreams are never wasted, and for helping to create the stories that ended up on these pages.

Thank you to Ty Stiklorius, Troy Carter, Zach Felber, Lee Loechler, Lillian Williams, Reid Hunter, Laxmi Vijay Sankar, David Gold, and the rest of the Atom Factory family for believing in our random ideas, including this book.

Thank you to our friend and first editor Natalli Ellsworth, for making sure we didn't embarrass ourselves in front of the bigwigs. And for leaving honest comments in the margins like, "You make a good point, but it reads a little like a middle school motivational poster."

Thank you to our agent Erin Malone for finding a home for our book baby, and the WME team for everything in between.

Thank you to our editor Jeremie Ruby-Strauss, for using the words "hilarious and moving" to describe our book proposal, and for taking a chance on two rookies. Thank you to Nina Cordes for answering all our e-mails with lightning speed, and for sounding excited to speak with us on the phone that one time. Also to Gallery's Louise Burke, Jen Bergstrom, Kristin Dwyer, Liz Psaltis,

Diana Velasquez, Jennifer Weidman, and copy editor Dominick Montalto.

Thank you to my husband, Austin (Brooke speaking), who has never doubted a single dream I ask him to chase with me. And to my clients, family, and friends who willingly took a backseat to this book for the past few years of my life.

Thank you to my manager, Adina Friedman (Lindsey speaking), who is always in my corner, forever, no matter what. And thank you to the loyal friends whom I bothered repeatedly for memories and old photos.

Thank you to every member of my crew for your time, talents, and friendship.

Thank you to the brilliant photographers whose art contributed to this book: Robin Roemer, Leavitt Wells, Adam Elmakias, Mikael Hakali, Amy Harris, Katie Rich, Jon D. Barker, Tim Tronckoe, Ray Shum, Nicole Fara Silver, Timothy Nguyen, Sharolyn Lindsay, and Annie Randall Pratt.

Thank you to these beautiful people for the endless love and support: Jennifer Stirling, Marina Inagaki, Vova Stirling, Erich Jackson, Jason Gaviati, Drew Steen, Michelle Miller, Keri Latta, Leslie Landers, Whitney Marcum, Janet Willis, Lilly Singh, Janelle Scott, Matt Ang, and Meghan Camarena.

And a special thanks to the Wi-Fi connections around the world that made our late-night, post-show, delirious book writing sessions possible. We owe you one.

PHOTO
CREDITS

PHOTO INSERT
CAPTIONS
AND CREDITS

Page 1

Top left: © Timothy Nguyen Photography

Top right: Photo by Ray Shum

Left, second from top: © Timothy Nguyen Photography

Right, second from top: Courtesy of Janelle Huopalainen

Left, second from bottom: © Timothy Nguyen Photography

Center, second from bottom: Mikael Hakali Photography

Bottom left: Photography by Nicole Fara Silver

Bottom right: Mikael Hakali Photography

Page 2

Top left: Photo by Katie Rich

Top right: Mikael Hakali Photography

Left, second from top: Mikael Hakali Photography

Left, second from bottom: Mikael Hakali Photography

Center right: Photography by Tim Tronckoe (www.timtronckoe.com)

Bottom left: Photography by Nicole Fara Silver

Bottom right: Photography by Tim Tronckoe (www.timtronckoe.com)

Page 3

Top left: Courtesy of Jani Dix

Top right: Disneyland with the family

Courtesy of the author

Left, second from top: Behind The Scenes for "Dragon Age"
Courtesy of the author
Center, second from top: With my Mission companion/college roommate,
Kaitlyn, before the mud run
Courtesy of Devin Graham
Right, second from top: Photography by Tim Tronckoe (www.timtronckoe.com)
Left, second from bottom: College rainbow costume
Courtesy of the author
Bottom left: Adam Elmakias Photography
Bottom center: Adam Elmakias Photography
Bottom right: Courtesy of Adina Friedman

Page 4
Top left: Adam Elmakias Photography
Top right: My trusty travel companion—compliments of a lovely fan
Courtesy of Adina Friedman
Left, second from top: Pre-show prayer
Adam Elmakias Photography
Right, second from top: Red carpet with my boys
Courtesy of Adina Friedman
Left, second from bottom: With my Mission companion/college roommate,
Kaitlyn, after the mud run
Courtesy of Devin Graham
Right, second from bottom: Photo by Ray Shum
Bottom left: Adam Elmakias Photography
Bottom right: My dad's book launch party
Courtesy of the author

Page 5
Top left: Whitney and me in Paris during my first European tour
Courtesy of Erich Jackson
Top right: The girls and me at Disneyland our senior year of high school
Courtesy of Amy Williamson
Left, second from top: Brooke's first day on tour with me as my wardrobe
extraordinaire
Courtesy of Adina Friedman

Right, second from top: An important phone call with my tour manager, Erich
Courtesy of the author
Left, second from bottom: Adam Elmakias Photography
Right, second from bottom: My sisters and me at Brooke's wedding
Annie Randall Photography
Bottom left: My tour bestie and makeup wonder woman, Michelle Miller
Photo by Amy Harris
Bottom right: Mikael Hakali Photography

Page 6
Top left: Mikael Hakali Photography
Top right: Mikael Hakali Photography
Middle left: Adam Elmakias Photography
Middle right: Photo by Lee Loechler
Bottom left: Photography by Tim Tronckoe (www.timtronckoe.com)
Bottom center: Photo by Ray Shum
Bottom right: Photograph by Jon D. Barker (@jondbarker on social media)

Page 7
Top left: Adam Elmakias Photography
Top right: Photo by Ray Shum
Middle left: Photo by Amy Harris
Middle right: Photo by Amy Harris
Bottom left: Courtesy of Leavitt Wells / Leave it to Leavitt Photography
Bottom center: Mikael Hakali Photography
Bottom right: Mikael Hakali Photography

Page 8
Top left: Photo by Katie Rich
Top right: Mikael Hakali Photography
Left, second from top: © Timothy Nguyen Photography
Center: Mikael Hakali Photography
Left, second from bottom: Photo by Ray Shum
Middle right: Courtesy of Leavitt Wells / Leave it to Leavitt Photography
Bottom left: Courtesy of Leavitt Wells / Leave it to Leavitt Photography
Bottom right: Courtesy of Leavitt Wells / Leave it to Leavitt Photography